Advance Praise

"aj crabill's Our Tools They Deserve *presents a transformative argument for addressing student behavior through mindset rather than punishment, challenging the traditional reliance on out-of-school suspensions. In this insightful work, crabill emphasizes the crucial role of adult mindset in schools, complementing the typical focus on knowledge and skills. He suggests that a belief in every student's ability to overcome challenges is key to unlocking their potential.*

"*crabill invites educators and school leaders to rethink whether students are truly feeling a sense of belonging and connection or simply conforming to rules without the necessary tools for success. He lays out strategies that prioritize changing adult behaviors in order to foster environments where students can thrive.*

"*For anyone dedicated to the belief that all children can succeed,* Our Tools They Deserve *is an essential read. It offers valuable insights into how intentional shifts in adult attitudes and practices can lead to improved student outcomes, making it a must-read for school leaders, school-based teams, and anyone involved in shaping the lives of children.*"

–**Joe Gothard**, Superintendent,
Madison Metropolitan School District

"*It's not every day that you find a resource that truly transforms how we think about changing the culture and climate of our schools and communities.* Our Tools They Deserve *is that resource—a guide that sheds light on the knowledge, skills, and mindset needed to create a positive, safe, and thriving environment where student voices are genuinely heard. This book will challenge your perspectives, prompting reflection on your role in fostering an equitable and inclusive community.*

"*I was introduced to aj crabill through our district's strategic planning process, and his approach to improving our culture and climate was both inspiring and practical. His unique ability to tailor information to various audiences—whether it's high-level administrators or energetic students—*

makes complex concepts accessible and engaging. With his guidance, our district successfully launched a student-led restorative practices initiative, which has now been building community and transforming mindsets for three years.

"aj's excitement and command of the subject are contagious, and now, through this book, he brings his wisdom to a wider audience. Our Tools They Deserve *is a must-read for anyone seeking to shift their mindset and embrace practices that center student leadership and restorative values. I am thrilled that readers will have the opportunity to learn from his insights and, like us, be inspired to make lasting change."

–Kim Saunders, Climate and Culture Systems Consultant, Columbus City Schools

"If you are looking for a book that will change lives, you are in the right place. If you are looking for a book that will teach you how to pour into kids in ways that will empower their futures, you are in the right place. If you are looking for a book that can head off the violence in our schools and communities and teach kids how to be better members of society, you are in the right place. The work isn't short term. And it isn't easy. And it takes commitment and heart. But it has to start somewhere. If you are ready for it to start with you, you are in the right place.

"I met aj crabill when he was Deputy Commissioner for Education for Texas. He had done a presentation about restorative practices for the Houston Independent School District, which my principal had attended. I had started a new group at my school called PALs, the focus of which was to change school culture through mediation and accountability. My principal asked aj to lead a course for our new PALs and that ultimately set the direction for our program. It was an unbelievable chance encounter that changed the lives of 16 kids who were then able to influence many kids who were struggling with good decision making. All they needed were the tools and the encouragement. And now you have the opportunity to teach kids how to facilitate change on your campus.

"The question is, Is it worth it? After 32 years in the classroom, it is more worth it than anything else I have taught. And now you have that opportunity too. You can change the lives of kids. And the ripple effects will be more far-reaching than you will ever know."

–Mari Ritchie, Teacher, Houston Independent School District

"aj crabill's Our Tools They Deserve *is a must read for policy makers and administrative leaders. Taking on the adult mindset in schools that impact how *we educate, support, and develop the next generation of student scholars by going beyond the typical myopic focus on only skills and knowledge. Based on his decades as an elected school board member, state level deputy commissioner in charge of governance, and practical experience in training thousands of school system teams, crabill's practice is grounded and applicable. I could not recommend Our Tools They Deserve any more emphatically."*

–**Richard A. Carranza**, Chanceller Emeritus, New York City Public Schools

"I worked with aj for many years and had the honor of witnessing first hand the impact he has on young people. AJ has an incredible gift for seeing the very best in each student. By pushing them out of their comfort zone he helps them see they are capable of more than they ever dreamed. He challenges both students and educators to build their community, be leaders and to 'be the change they want to see.' aj is a visionary and a true gift to the world of education."

–**Renee Schultz**, Director of Campus Ministry, St. Teresa's Academy

"Every child deserves the chance to live the life Jesus created for them—to serve, grow, and share their unique gifts with the world. This work is transformative, and its impact is profound, not only for our students but for our schools and communities. When we prioritize the needs of our students above the wants of adults, we unlock their full potential. If we're dissatisfied with the behavior of our students, we must look in the mirror—what we see is often a reflection of our own actions and attitudes. This book challenges adults to shift their mindset, empowering us to become the change that our students so deeply deserve."

–**Georgina Perez**, Former Member, Texas State Board of Education

"Our Tools They Deserve: Why Adults Choose Retribution, How Students Can Practice Restoration, is a powerful read. I love this book because it challenges us as educators, as adults, as power brokers to elevate student voice while coaching them to use tools that will benefit them not only now, but throughout life. This is a must read for anyone who truly wants to make a difference in the lives of children."

–**Crystal L. Hill**, Superintendent, Charlotte (NC) Mecklenburg Schools

"The mindset shifts outlined in this book have the potential to transform our culture. Empowering our young people to "be the change" is exactly what the world needs right now. Kudos to AJ for not only investing in this work, but reflecting on and writing about it so educators everywhere and the learners in our care (aka our future leaders) can benefit from his brilliant strategies."

–**Linda Amici**, Instructional Coach, Westerville (OH) City Schools

"What appeared to be a silly role play exercise, taught me a great deal about self-awareness. It's more than what you say; It is how you say it, which includes body language. Restorative practice starts with oneself by identifying how different situations make us feel. Understanding what upsets me has taught me how to address situations. This lesson teaches students how to address their feelings before they act."

–**Magali Rojas**, Former Specialist, El Centro

"aj crabill's book is a must read for educators and policymakers committed to building inclusive, empathetic and transformative learning environments. It opens with the inspiring journey of Jasmine, a student once labeled as violent, who transforms into a leader and peer mediator through the shift from retributive to restorative practices. The narrative challenges the idea that students like Jasmine are inherently problematic, revealing instead that what they often lack is the right support to navigate their challenges.

"The book emphasizes the importance of self-regulation, empathy, and accountability rather than punishment. By showcasing Jasmine's success and the wider impact of student-led approaches, the author makes a compelling case for schools to rethink their responses to student behavior.

"More than just a call to action, the book provides a practical blueprint for implementing restorative practices that foster connection, belonging, and growth by making a compelling case for educators to change the default mindset in schools. It serves as a beacon for educators and leaders, guiding them towards a more compassionate education system where every student is seen, valued, and supported to reach their full potential."

–**Jaime Aquino**, Superintendent, San Antonio Independent School District

"*Our Tools, They Deserve* is an innovative exploration of student restorative practices that inspires young people to take charge of their educational experiences. This critical book provides practical tools and strategies while emphasizing the importance of student agency in fostering a positive school culture. It empowers students to speak up for themselves and their peers, promoting a more inclusive and supportive educational environment. It is a must-read for both educators and students."

–**Talisa Dixon**, Former Superintendent, Columbus (OH) City Schools

"Dynamic, bold and impactful, the first two chapters of Our Tools They Deserve by aj crabill offer a fresh look at why retributive approaches are so common in schools. crabill encourages readers to rethink how we manage behavior, focusing on how what we know, what we can do, and how these realities we face impact the choices we make as educators. These opening chapters set the stage for a shift toward a student-led restorative approach, pushing communities to choose strategies that help children develop the tools they need to reach their full potential. crabill's message is clear: it's not just about adults using these data-driven techniques, but also about giving students the chance to practice them, too."

–**Dr. Grenita Lathan**, Superintendent, Springfield (MO) Public Schools

"For years, the intention of serving all students has been the mantle taken by educators. The contents of Our Tools They Deserve provides practical steps that take the quaint saying—serving all students—into concrete actions that will lead to improved school culture and student outcomes. Moreover, the prescription shared delivers beyond today. Executing this playbook will equip and empower students with tools to succeed, generate an understanding of their own agency, and students young people the opportunity to realize the dreams that otherwise would have been unattainable."

–**Jeff Cottrill**, CEO & Superintendent, IDEA Public Schools

"I have known aj since 2019, when we first met while both consulting for a large urban district in the Midwest. I was impressed by the depth of his knowledge in and dedication to making education the transformative force it should be for improving lives. This initial interaction with aj was as he was supplying this school district support in Board governance.

"As we worked together, he shared with me his passion for student-led restorative practice and its potential to alter individuals and cultures for true change. This caught my attention as I was just beginning to form my own consultancy about student agency. I was afforded the opportunity to watch AJ work with 70 urban teenagers from various high schools, often rival ones at that, unassisted by any other adults. This was mind blowing!

"aj's time with these students, who spanned the discipline, academic, and racial continuum, took place over three seven-hour days. The change in these kids was real and life-giving, most importantly to the students themselves, but also, and importantly, to their schools. I subsequently committed to getting aj in front of more crowds about this work, as well as to documenting his work via film.

"I can't recommend aj's talents about SLRP strongly enough. The tools and dispositions that are part of the SLRP experience are invaluable for all who learn and use them!"
  —**Mike Nicholson**, Founder, Learning InspirED / Student Power Summit

"In his latest book, aj crabill does a magnificent job of identifying the tools that students need to change their behavior for everyone's benefit. Part of the magic is clearly defining complex words in a concise manner for clear understanding. Many people assume they know these meanings. Good things happen by design, not accident. The design and content of the book will lead to the transformation of the lives of students and adults! Bravo!"
  —**Michael Hinojosa**, Former Superintendent, Dallas Independent School District

"Our Tools They Deserve introduces the essential tools students need to successfully navigate challenging situations. Typically, school systems adopt a punitive approach to student discipline, often adhering to 'Codes of Conduct' that don't work. However, after reading this book, it becomes clear that by investing time in teaching students how to use these tools, they can transform from 'worst-behaved' to 'impressive students.'

"The book equips adults with the mindsets and tools needed to approach discipline challenges differently, thereby maximizing positive student behavior and academic outcomes. It offers educators a new model that allows students to anticipate future challenges, reflect on their choices, and consider the potential positive or negative outcomes before taking action on a decision. The book also includes helpful tables that summarize the framework for a deeper understanding. It provides adults with alternatives to removing students from the learning environment. The content of Our Tools They Deserve creates a win-win support system for everyone."
  —**Laura Stout**, Former Division Superintendent, Houston Independent School District / Chief School Improvement Officer, K-12 Leadership Diagnostics, LLC

Our Tools They Deserve

Why Adults Choose Retribution, How Students Can Practice Restoration

airick journey crabill

Copyright © 2024 airick journey crabill
All rights reserved.

STUDENT-LED RESTORATIVE PRACTICES

Our Tools They Deserve: Why Adults Choose Retribution, How Students Can Practice Restoration

No part of this publication may be reproduced, distributed, or transmitted in any form or by any means, electronic or mechanical, including photocopying, recording, or by any information storage and retrieval without the prior written permission of the author, except for the inclusion of brief quotations in critical reviews and certain other non-commercial uses permitted by copyright law. For permission, please contact the author.

Special note: while the stories discussed in this book are based on real-life interactions, all names of children/students have been changed to protect the privacy of the young people involved.

ISBN:
978-1-964014-45-6 Paperback
978-1-964014-46-3 Hardback
978-1-964014-47-0 Ebook

Published services provided by Tasfil Publishing LLC
Voorhees, New Jersey

Library of Congress Control Number: 2024920731.

Dedication

My first book, *Great On Their Behalf,* is about school systems becoming responsive to the needs of students, but this book is about the tools that allow students to thrive even when systems are not responsive. This book is written for and dedicated to:

1. The students who experienced being thrown away and given up on by adults around them and yet still managed to be a rose in the concrete
2. The students who are still in the struggle and for whom this work can provide more fertile earth in which to grow.

Contents

Introduction 1

Part I: Why Adults Choose Retribution 11

    Chapter 1: Knowledge-Based Reasons 13
    Chapter 2: Skill-Based Reasons 23
    Chapter 3: Mindset-Based Reasons 39

Part II: How Students Can Practice Restoration 49

Step One: Focus Mindset 51

    Chapter 4: Maximization 53
    Chapter 5: Trust 61
    Chapter 6: Choice 67

Step Two: Commit Leadership 73

    Chapter 7: School System Leadership 75
    Chapter 8: School-Based Leadership 83

Step Three: Clarify and Monitor Priorities 91

    Chapter 9: Setting Goals 93
    Chapter 10: Monitor What Matters 101

Step Four: Practice Community Circles 107

    Chapter 11: Creating Belonging 109
    Chapter 12: Implementing Community Circles 113

Step Five: Practice Mediation Circles 119

    Chapter 13: Creating Connection 121
    Chapter 14: Implementing Mediation Circles 125

Step Six: Practice Restorative Circles 133

    Chapter 15: Creating Reparation 135
    Chapter 16: Implementing Restorative Circles 141

Part III: Continuous Improvement..149
    Chapter 17: Next Steps 151
    Chapter 18: Challenges and Strategies 159

Appendix 169

Additional Resources 169

Gratitudes..173

About the Author...175

Introduction

To Hammer a Screw

"I have you on speakerphone with several of my administrators," the principal said, which explained the echoing sound quality, "and I'd like to visit with you about Jasmine."

"What happened?" I asked, immediately on high alert.

Jasmine had been in our summer program and, like many of our students, had a rather extensive discipline history. The principal had asked if we'd enroll her in our summer program after she was in a fight on the last day of school. She had beaten up two girls—at the same time. Apparently, she'd been suspended every year since middle school for fighting and showed no sign of slowing down. Instead of punishing her with the usual disciplinary response, the principal had called us because she was looking for ways to help Jasmine be successful.

The day Jasmine arrived at our program, she was true to form: she rapidly proceeded to pick a fight with one of the smaller boys. I came across them just in time to prevent it from escalating. That was our formal introduction.

"Well," the principal began, "we had a whole Jasmine-intervention plan for today, since it was the first day of school. The plan was that as soon as we saw a crowd start to gather, we'd rush in quickly. One of us would grab Jasmine high, and one would grab her low. Another would pull the other student away."

I had a feeling she was shaking her head in exasperation.

"Sure enough," she continued, "tensions started to rise, and a crowd started to form. I looked up to see Jasmine moving at full speed toward the middle of the crowd. So I signaled to everyone to get in there and break it up before it began. But we were too slow. We tried to get close enough to grab her, but the crowd closed in too fast." I heard a small laugh escape her lips, and I silently wondered if she was on the verge of losing it.

"This is where things get strange," she said, openly chuckling at this point. "By the time we got into the middle of the crowd, Jasmine was there. She was standing between two girls who looked like they were squared off to fight each other, but she had them both doing breathing exercises. She de-escalated the fight!"

Now *I was* laughing out loud, mostly because over the summer I watched Jasmine practicing self-regulation and other vital skills in preparation for this very moment.

"What, exactly, happened this summer?" the principal asked, sounding completely befuddled.

There was nothing wrong with Jasmine. She was not an evil person. She was not mean spirited, and she was not particularly angry or violent by nature. Clearly that was how she had been behaving, but it was not who she was. Her behavior stemmed from her lacking the tools necessary to successfully navigate the challenges she encountered.

How can I be absolutely confident about stating Jasmine's problem was related to her lack of tools? Because for nearly two decades, we've witnessed many students do what Jasmine did: arrive without tools, behaving one way, and later leave with new tools, behaving another way. Why? Because the reality is this: students can consistently be relied upon to use the most optimal tool in their toolbox to address whatever circumstance they face.

If you ever see a child trying to hammer a screw into a piece of wood with a wrench, the most accurate assessment isn't that they're bad or dumb or disobedient. It's that they lack a screwdriver or fluency with using one. Cure that, and watch as they—without prompting, without cajoling, without threatening, without punishing—switch to screwing in the screw with a screwdriver. That children begin life lacking knowledge about tools or the skills with which to use them is not their fault; that they remain that way is ours.

We spent the summer teaching Jasmine specific tools. Initially, the tools we taught her were about accountability, responsibility, self-regulation, metacognition, active listening, and empathy, and then ultimately around belonging, connection, and reparation. This book is about how to make these tools—the knowledge of them and the skill to use them—available to more of our students rather than throwing students away for using inappropriate tools.

Full of pride and joy, I explained to the principal: "Jasmine is just using the tools we taught her."

Introduction

Retributive Practices and Restorative Practices

The principal, too, was full of pride and joy. Pride because she chose to risk taking a new approach—instead of seeking retribution for Jasmine's fighting, she got her support—and joy because it paid off. That decision wasn't an easy one. Something we must all wrestle with is that in our hearts, we often desire retribution. We are animated by our desire to evaluate the harm that we perceive has occurred and then mete out an equal measure of harm in retaliation. And I know *why* we do it: to teach our children, to help them learn responsibility, to train them in knowing right from wrong. But I invite you to consider that this is largely a story we invent to justify the desire for retribution that lives in our hearts. Our society is steeped in it. Our neighborhoods are run by it. And when we are not careful, our schools are ruined by it. This is what we do in large part, I suspect, because this is what we know; it is what was done to us. We reproduce that which we were trained in. In other words, by nature, retribution is our default.

It's vital to clarify that while retributive practices are not good or bad, right or wrong, they are an intentional approach to how people are in community with one another. Restorative practices are a different approach. My invitation to schools is to not simply fall into default behavior, but rather to choose the appropriate tools for the situation.

- **Retributive practices** describe a spectrum of tools that emphasize **compliance** as the context for community, **authority** as the response to conflict, and, when harm is created, **punishment** as the consequence.
- **Restorative practices** describe a spectrum of tools that emphasize **belonging** as the context for community, **connection** as the response to conflict, and, when harm is created, **reparation** as the consequence.

While we will unpack these differences throughout the book, it's important to clarify upfront that I'm not an absolutist about this. I don't believe that retributive practices are bad/wrong while restorative practices are good/right. I believe in the use of retributive practices in certain contexts and at times have been the wielder of them in my official capacities.

The opportunity that I lift up is that in many moments when we are defaulting to retributive practices in our schools, we are actually making it harder to accomplish the intention of schools. That is, when we repeatedly remove students from school without a plan for supporting them in acquiring the tools they need, we make it harder to improve student outcomes. Instead, my invitation is that restorative practices can be the default approach, and, only when circumstances warrant it, schools can choose to fall back on retributive practices as a secondary or tertiary strategy. The word I use to summarize why I advocate for restorative practices as the default rather than retributive practices as the default is maximization.

Maximization

"Thank you for telling Jasmine to stop fighting! I never imagined that would work," the principal said.

"Actually, we don't tell students to stop fighting. Never have; likely never will. There's nothing wrong with the skill of fighting. It's just a tool. But like any tool, it matters when and where you use it. We simply taught her other tools and made this request: when confronted with situations at school, self-regulate first, and then choose whichever tool you believe to be most appropriate to the situation. If it's fighting, so be it. There will be consequences, but so be it. If fighting isn't the best tool, however, then pick whichever one is, and use it."

There was silence on the other end of the line.

"I know it sounds strange," I continued. "But it sounds like you're seeing the results for yourself. As to more details about what happened this summer? Ask Jasmine. I'm guessing she can't wait to share."

That year, with the principal's full support, Jasmine didn't only share about her summer; she went on to start a peer mediation team at her school. She was the team president and brought me in to co-lead training for a group of her classmates. The more they conducted peer mediations, the more practice she and her classmates received with their new tools. The circumstances surrounding Jasmine's life didn't radically shift, but the tools she had fluency with did. As a result, she was never suspended again. She never fought at school again. By the end of the year, despite all odds and given her previous behavioral and academic records, she graduated.

When I attended her graduation, her mother came up to me and handed me a letter. Later that night, I teared up reading it.

> *I had accepted that I would lose my daughter to violence. I just knew something bad was going to happen because of how she acted. But now things are different. I feel hopeful. I feel*

Introduction

> *like I have my daughter back for the first time. Thank you.*

Our work is merely a catalyst. We can't possibly be surprised when, lacking the tools we want a child to be able to choose from, they choose a tool they already have. This work opens students to begin to see themselves and what's possible for their lives in a new way. Inside of this new view of life—a view aided by the tools this work develops—new openings for being arise that create new openings for doing. What is remarkable about Jasmine was always within her—remarkable things ready to be built. She simply lacked the tools with which to do so.

What I want—what I suspect we all want for our children—is *maximization*: that they experience the maximal expression of who they are capable of being as a growing, sentient, sapient individual. By doing so, they can live a choice-filled life on their own terms in which they are able to care for themselves, their loved ones, and their communities.

But I don't just want maximization for the young people I work with. I want it for every child everywhere. My bet is that since you are reading this book, you do too. So the question I invite you to consider now is: when a student is acting in an unacceptable manner, as Jasmine was, which path is more effective at creating the possibility of maximization: finding a way to kick her out of school for ten days or finding a way to get her the tools she deserves?

Adult-Led and Student-Led

My intention is to ensure the opportunity for maximization for all our students. This will require them to possess the tools necessary to live a choice-filled life. Academics are certainly a critical part of this process, but so are tools like accountability, responsibility, self-regulation, metacognition, active listening, and empathy. My experience is that when students have these tools and have gained fluency with them, they make different choices than they otherwise would if they lacked these specific tools.

If we want to increase the likelihood that students gain these tools, then it's not enough for them to participate in the conversations born of restorative practices. It's not even enough that they simply attend a summer program like mine where they learn restorative practices tools. They must become the keepers of the restorative practices themselves. The more students practice the tools while leading this work with their classmates, the more they strengthen these skills within themselves. I am not opposed to adult-led restorative practices—any movement toward restorative practices in schools as the default approach increases the likelihood of maximization. But my aspiration for our society isn't only that our students experience restoration; it's that they can generate it for themselves. That is accelerated more by a student-led approach rather than an adult-led approach.

Jasmine and her classmates led the peer mediation work throughout her senior year. Once an adult would identify a disruptive student and have them pulled out of class, Jasmine would step in to navigate the conflict and then sending the students back to class. Each mediation they led was an opportunity for them, as students, to build their fluency with the tools we taught them while protecting the learning environment for the other students. As a vital feature of this approach, having students work with other students in these situations meant that teachers weren't being asked to stop providing instruction; teachers were able to keep teaching while students kept learning.

I want our children to learn accountability for their actions, not disassociated punishment based on having frustrated an adult. But I also want to create the conditions wherein they are actively cultivating the tools necessary to create community at will, to restore connection at will, and to repair harm at will. Just as much as the academic skills we will nurture within them, these tools—once they're developed by the students leading the work within the practice-rich environment of their schools—will assist them in being able to lovingly navigate a world often populated by hurting and hurtful humans.

From Retributive to Restorative

There are no easy answers or quick-fix solutions in this book, and in the end, you will have to evaluate for yourself whether a default retributive approach or restorative approach is more effective at creating the outcomes you want for your school. That said, this book is about a student-led restorative approach to addressing behavior, not because this approach is right and other approaches are wrong but because a student-led restorative approach expedites adults and students alike along the path toward maximization.

Such a radical shift requires equally significant changes in adult behavior. Such things are not effortless, so this book focuses on three key drivers of adult behavior change as a guide: knowledge, skill, and mindset. Knowledge is what you know. Skill is what you can do with what you know. Mindset is how you view the world. While shifts in all three are typically needed to make the adult

Introduction

behavior transition from retributive to restorative, by far the most potent of these three is mindset.

> **Knowledge** describes what someone knows.
> **Skill** describes what someone can do with what they know.
>
> **Mindset** describes someone's interpretation of the world—the lens through which they make meaning of what they are experiencing.

Circles

Restorative practices look at the spectrum of behaviors and attempt to pair those behaviors with responses that are appropriately tailored to the needs the behaviors are surfacing. Among the most common restorative responses is the use of circles—intentional gatherings of the relevant parties who come together to address the needs of the individuals and the group. Just as the behaviors in a school will be quite varied, the available restorative practice responses need to be varied as well.

It can be helpful to think of the spectrum of behaviors as ranging from calm to violent, with the resulting energy being from zero to ten. At various steps along that spectrum, different restorative practices are used to support the needs of the parties involved. For example, if two people are both fives toward each other, with behaviors that range from high conflict to low harm, then the ideal response might be a mediation circle. Behavior reveals needs; needs reveal ideal responses. The following illustration shows some examples of how this spectrum might exist in a school. Each school needs to create this continuum of behaviors and responses for itself as part of its student-led restorative practices guide.

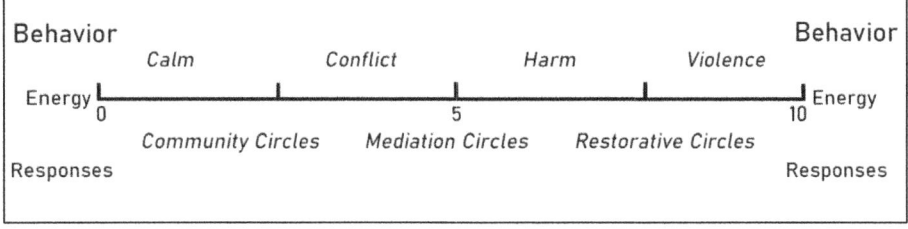

To guide schools along this journey, this book walks through our default reliance on retribution and why it is so pervasive in Part I: Why Adults Choose Retribution:

> Knowledge-Based Reasons: What do school system leaders and school leaders not know that leads to retribution as the default?
>
> Skill-Based Reasons: What are school system leaders and school leaders unable to do, the lack of which is steering them toward retributive practices?
>
> Mindset-Based Reasons: What harmful ways of seeing the world have school system leaders and school leaders unknowingly adopted that minimize students' chance at maximization?

Understanding how we got here is important, but it doesn't cause us to go somewhere new. The adoption of student-led restorative practices is a challenging road that requires clear implementation steps. That is the intention of Part II: How Students Can Practice Restoration:

> Step One: Focus Mindset: School system leaders and school leaders align behaviors with improving student outcomes, starting with their own behaviors.
>
> Step Two: Commit Leadership: Restorative leadership teams are created and guide the implementation of restorative practices.
>
> Step Three: Clarify and Monitor Priorities: Restorative leadership teams work collaboratively to develop goals and self-evaluate.
>
> Step Four: Practice Community Circles: Restorative leadership teams guide the use of circles focused on creating the experience of belonging.
>
> Step Five: Practice Mediation Circles: Restorative leadership teams guide the use of circles focused on creating connection when conflict exists.
>
> Step Six: Practice Restorative Circles: Restorative leadership teams guide the use of circles focused on repairing harm that has been created.

Our Tools They Deserve

As communities make the choice of which strategy to use, my recommendation—the ultimate intention of this book—is that we seek whichever path is most aligned with providing the children of our community with the tools they need to experience maximization. As a community, our tools can be used to forge a path toward maximization, or they can just as easily be used to disrupt it. Rather than only relying on adults to use these tools, this

Introduction

book further calls on us to confer these tools, and the circumstances of their use, to our students so that they can begin to gain fluency with them as well. Maximization of human potential describes the intention behind adults sharing our tools they deserve.

Part I
Why Adults Choose Retribution

Chapter 1:
Knowledge-Based Reasons

Restorative Practices and Retributive Practices

It is common for us to begin describing restorative practices and then for school system staff to ask sincerely and innocently: "isn't restorative what we already do?" The question proves that many school staff immediately resonate with the concept. But it also reveals that many do not know the difference between restorative practices and retributive practices. This is the first and most common reason I've discovered that school systems are not yet engaged in restorative practices.

In the Introduction, I shared the following:

- **Restorative practices** describe a spectrum of tools that emphasize **belonging** as the context for community, **connection** as the response to conflict, and, when harm is created, **reparation** as the consequence.
- **Retributive practices** describe a spectrum of tools that emphasize **compliance** as the context for community, **authority** as the response to conflict, and, when harm is created, **punishment** as the consequence.

Because a deep understanding of these ideas is necessary before reading the rest of this book, let's clear up some common misconceptions that often lead to choosing a retributive approach.

Misconceptions About Harm

Throughout this book, I am very specific about what I mean when I discuss certain terms. In few places is that more the case than with the word *harm*. But understanding harm requires understanding the ideas that surround it.

The first of these is the idea of *homeostasis*. The way I explain homeostasis to students is that it describes physical and emotional stability and regulation in one's environment. When I am at rest—not exerting myself in any way, whether physically, mentally, emotionally—then I might say that I'm in a state of homeostasis. This isn't good or bad or right or wrong; it's just a person being in a state of stability and regulation. A key understanding is that living things naturally seek homeostasis (more on that to come).

> **Homeostasis** describes the physical and emotional stability and regulation in one's environment.

The next idea is *stress*. Stress has a bad reputation, but when I refer to stress, I'm simply describing when a trigger results in someone being out of homeostasis. When I'm sitting down, I'm generally in homeostasis. When I go for a jog, my body is no longer in homeostasis. I'm placing stress on my body by jogging. Because of this, the act of jogging triggers my body to begin processes with the intention of restoring homeostasis: I sweat to cool down. My heart speeds up to deliver more oxygen. And so forth. When I stop jogging, slowly my body—as is the tendency with living things—returns to homeostasis.

That's a physical example, but emotional examples work similarly. When I'm emotionally in homeostasis and then someone sneaks up and startles me, that causes stress; it temporarily takes me out of homeostasis. In response to this trigger, my body begins processes with the intention of restoring homeostasis: my adrenaline might spike to prepare me to protect myself. My heart races again. And so on. When the surprise dies down, however, slowly my body calms again and returns to homeostasis.

> **Stress** describes when a trigger results in someone being out of homeostasis.

I find it incredibly helpful for students to know about homeostasis as a way to access metacognition about their current state of being. The more that students can reflect on what is happening to them in the moment by naming the physical and emotional experiences they are having, the greater degree of self-regulation they can demonstrate when they are experiencing stress.

Stress isn't inherently good or bad or right or wrong. It is a natural process that happens when we are out of homeostasis. In the case of jogging, I intentionally cause stress in my body because of the benefits it brings. When I work out with weights, I'm intentionally stressing my muscles because of the benefits it brings.

As people, we likely experience stress quite regularly. In fact, at times stress can be helpful for us. A nudge outside of homeostasis, as when we are working out, can be exactly what we intend and need. The challenge is that, as with anything, too much of a useful thing can cease to be useful.

Harm describes what happens when stress results in physical or emotional damage that constrains the typical return to homeostasis. Said differently, when stress reaches a point that it degrades our ability to return to homeostasis, then the stress has become harmful. Harm is what happens when stress goes too far. And where normally the body naturally returns to homeostasis, once harm occurs—whether physical, emotional, or otherwise—it takes longer to return to homeostasis, if the body can even do so on its own. Depending on how acute the harm is, it may take additional external support to return to homeostasis.

> **Harm** describes what happens when stress that results in physical or emotional damage that constrains the typical return to homeostasis.

It is inappropriate for harm to be created and for there to *not* be a consequence—a response of some sort. Now the reason for that is clearer: *if it's hard for homeostasis to return on its own because harm has been created, and there is no consequence aimed at repairing the harm, then the results of the harm may linger and eventually even become permanent.* This is why, when harm is created, it is inappropriate for there not to be a response – inappropriate for there not to be some type of consequence. The default retributive consequence for addressing harm is punishment; the default restorative consequence for addressing harm is reparation.

It's also worth clarifying that while stress describes the experience of being triggered out of homeostasis, unfortunately, many people confuse stress with trauma and confuse trauma with harm. Or just as problematically, they confuse the experience of trauma with being caused by a trigger. Each of these is a way of viewing trauma that is less likely to inspire maximization, so let's get some clarity around those terms.

Trauma is related to stress in that trauma describes when the experience of stress exceeds a person's coping tools. Trauma is related to harm in that harm often triggers stress, which, if it exceeds someone's coping tools, can lead to trauma. But this is a radically different understanding of trauma than is often used. This view of trauma better explains why providing students with tools is so essential and why having students lead restorative practices as a way of gaining fluency with those tools is equally essential. Trauma doesn't result purely because a stressful incident occurs. Trauma results when a person's current tools are insufficient to help them cope with the incident.

> **Trauma** describes when the experience of stress—physical, social, or otherwise—exceeds coping tools, both internal and external.

This is why two people can have the exact same experience but for one it is traumatizing and for the other it is not. One of them lacked the coping tools they needed, while the other possessed them.

This view of trauma is essential because a common view—that events are the sole cause of trauma—leads to adults attempting to surround children with emotional bubble wrap so that no uncomfortable events happen. Inside this common view of trauma, the way to prepare children for life isn't to prepare them; it's to make sure that life doesn't happen to them in the first place. But what's equally problematic about this view of trauma is that it negates the idea of teaching tools: if trauma is unavoidable once a traumatizing event happens, then why bother teaching students how to grow and access their internal and external coping tools. If events are what caused trauma, it would be more energetically economical to try to prevent such events.

In addition, this common view of trauma leads us to do the exact opposite of a restorative approach: it encourages us to aggressively punish anyone who causes a potentially traumatizing event. I'm not talking about illegal, violent, or unethical behavior; those warrant a different conversation. I'm talking about behavior that makes someone uncomfortable or viewpoints that someone doesn't like or expressions that might land in a way that causes someone to feel sad when they hear them. These behaviors become criminalized when our belief is that they cause trauma. But they don't cause trauma by themselves; inadequate access to the tools to cope with them does.

Punishment and Reparation

In our work, we are strongly committed to consequences—outcomes that occur in response to something happening—but not all consequences have identical effects. Reparation and punishment are two different types of consequences. Reparation as a consequence describes causing someone who created harm to engage in repairing the harm. Punishment as a consequence describes causing someone who created harm to experience equivalent harm. The difference is pivotal.

If our commitment is to punishment, our operational belief is that if we cause someone to experience harm in a dosage that is appropriate to the amount of harm they created, they will be taught not to create the same harm again, or the punishment will provide protection against future harm because they will have been removed (e.g., suspensions). Reread that sentence. We may not consciously think this is our theory, but this is exactly what we are doing when we engage in punishment. And as with the other concepts this book will discuss, I'm definitely not suggesting that punishment is good or bad or right or wrong. I'm describing the strategy, not judging it, because it is important for us to be open-eyed about which strategies we use to teach our students and why. Punishment as a consequence is a teaching strategy. So is reparation as a consequence.

With reparation, our operational belief is that if someone causes harm, them being responsible for getting present to the harm they created—for others, for the community, and for themselves—and then them being accountable for repairing that harm they created will teach them not to create the same harm again, and it will provide protection against future harm. Reparation is neither good or bad nor right or wrong; reparation as a consequence is a teaching strategy.

> **Consequence** describes an outcome that occurs in response to something happening.
>
> **Punishment** describes causing someone who created harm to experience equivalent harm.
>
> **Reparation** describes causing someone who created harm to engage in repairing the harm.

While both of these consequences—punishment and reparation—have pros and cons, my bias toward reparation as the default consequence for schools stems from its greater likelihood to create the conditions for maximization. Schools appear to believe that if we punish students swiftly and firmly enough, they'll behave. While this might have been true many decades ago, one of the most common types of school punishments we see now, suspensions, can often be used by students as an opportunity to play their favorite video games, message their friends at school, and contemplate how to get back at whoever they believe aggrieved them. Even if your belief is in punishment as a primary response, a response used in this manner does not accomplish the intentions of punishment.

Misconceptions About Conflict

Much like stress, conflict often has an undeserved negative connotation. Conflict describes the experience of interference between strategies for meeting needs. If I'm trying to get my needs met by walking up the steps and you're trying to get your needs met by walking down the steps, one way of interpreting the situation is that you are trying to prevent me from meeting my needs. But this is most often not the case. In my experience, it is actually rare that conflicts in schools emerge from two people being in opposition to each other. Rather, when we unpack it fully, we see the conflict is from the strategies we are using to meet our needs unintentionally interfering with each other. You're not trying to prevent me from meeting my needs; you're just walking down a flight of stairs. I'm not trying to prevent you from meeting your needs; I'm just walking up a flight of stairs.

Conflict is neither good or bad nor right or wrong; conflict is just conflict, and it's a normal part of being in a community with others. Conflicts will happen; that's not in question. What we do in moments of conflict tends to be what is decisive concerning whether we ultimately get our needs met or not. The default retributive approach to addressing conflict is authority; the default restorative approach to addressing conflict is connection.

Authority and Connection

Authority describes the power that is given to someone by a community. In an adult-led retributive approach to conflict, someone in a position of authority relative to the conflictants—the people in conflict—is called upon to listen to the details of the conflict and render a judgment. While there are many benefits to this approach to addressing conflict, maximization is not one of them. Nothing about an external authority imposing solutions today maximizes a student's ability to create solutions for themselves tomorrow; either we teach personal responsibility or we accept irresponsibility. Witnessing someone else develop and enforce a solution is not the same as having to assume the mental load to do so oneself. There is nothing wrong with using authority to address conflicts. It's just not a strategy for maximization.

Connection describes the choice to create and behave from a generous mindset about someone. When I feel connection with someone, my view of them—whether they have earned it or not—leads me to behave in ways that are mutually beneficial. The connection I have with my students leads me to see the best in them and to pull for the best from them. The connection I have with my colleagues drives me to create beneficial opportunities for them. The generosity of mindset inherent in connection has me behave in ways that seek out mutually beneficial solutions in moments of conflict. I'm looking for ways to get out of your way to make it easier for you to go down the stairs; maybe I'm going down the stairs with you to help ensure your needs get met. Experiencing connection with someone, and them with you, is a powerful gift.

When connection is present, even large conflicts seem manageable, but the converse is also true: in the absence of connection, even trivial conflicts seem insurmountable. When there are differing viewpoints, it is the lack of connection that creates discomfort rather than just the divergent views themselves. Connection is a social lubricant.

In a student-led restorative approach to conflict, the sole strategy is connection: create a space in which conflictants experience connection with each other. The intention is that in the space of connection, conflictants will find their own solutions, absent an external authority.

> **Conflict** describes the experience of interference between strategies for meeting needs.
>
> **Authority** describes the power that is given to someone by a community.
>
> **Connection** describes the choice to create and behave from a generous mindset about someone.
>
> **Conflictant** describes a person(s) involved in a conflict.

Again, connection as a strategy is not good or bad or right or wrong compared to authority as a strategy. They each have pros and cons. But connection as a strategy has a benefit that authority as a strategy does not: it places students on the path to maximization by supporting them in developing the tools necessary to effectively function independently in society. When schools choose authority as a strategy, it's often because it is viewed as more instructionally time efficient—and in the short term, it frequently is. Creating a conversation where conflictants come to experience connection can be quite time consuming. But when weighed against the decreased likelihood of escalating conflict, which can quickly lead to harmful behavior, supporting students to develop the tools necessary to address root causes can save dramatically more instructional time.

But this also speaks to why I am an adherent of student-led restorative practices rather than adult-led restorative practices. In addition to wanting students to develop skills around connection and conflict, I also don't want teachers spending their precious instructional time on every conflict. Teachers are already overworked and under-supported. Instead, having students lead connective conversations not only supports them with developing skill with their tools, but it relieves a burden on teachers that is harming their ability to focus on instruction.

Misconceptions About Community

Community describes a group of people formed with a shared characteristic. The experience of community can form around almost anything: people who live in the same area, drink the same drink, drive the same car, or even wear the same outfit. Membership in a community is conditional and is typically based upon possession of or identification with the shared characteristic. A school community is made up of everyone with one shared characteristic: they or a family member attend the school (e.g., families and students), work at the school (e.g., employees or volunteers), or in some way experience connection to the school (e.g., alumni or boosters).

School communities exist for one reason and one reason only: to improve student outcomes – to cause growth in what students know or are able to do. There are many things that school communities *do* but only one reason school communities *exist*. Any strategy that expands the experience of community within a school is likely to be in service to the reason that school communities exist–is likely to support improvements in student outcomes. Any strategy that impedes the experience of community needs to be utilized only when nothing else is available.

Compliance and Belonging

Compliance describes the choice to adhere to the expectations of authority. When students choose to comply with authority, the experience of community is created by the authority figure. For example, teachers create the experience of community in the classroom. This is not good or bad or right or wrong. It is worth noting, however, that the authority behind compliance is less likely to be derived from the consent of the governed—the students—but rather from their families/guardians, as children often are doing what their families have raised them to do. Therefore, for compliance to be effective, it often requires family agreements to be in alignment with educator agreements; this is not always going to be true. Additionally, given the inherent apartheid nature of schooling for children, where children are compliant because the authorities are making them be, they do not learn necessary tools for navigating the school environment that will help them in future communities. Meanwhile, when belonging is the context for community, students work collaboratively because they want to be part of the community.

Belonging describes the choice to create and behave from seeing others as having a generous mindset toward you. When someone experiences a sense of identification with a particular community, they might say, "I belong" in this particular community, meaning they feel seen and accepted by the people within that community. Belonging, as it turns out, is a very powerful phenomenon and is often positively and meaningfully correlated with a likelihood of persisting in school even when learning inevitably gets tough.

In addition, a student's experience of belonging to a peer group—and having that group become a major source of identity, even eclipsing the relationship they have with their families in some regards—is a developmentally normal and healthy process.

> **Community** describes a group of people formed with a shared characteristic.
>
> **Compliance** describes the choice to adhere to the expectations of authority.
>
> **Belonging** describes the choice to create and behave from seeing others as having a generous mindset toward you.

Belonging isn't good, bad, right, or wrong either; there are pros and cons to both strategies. But belonging does carry the correlational benefit of educational persistence that compliance does not. For this reason, I recommend the community-building strategy of belonging over the community-building strategy of compliance wherever it is practical to deploy.

Retributive and Restorative

All of this brings us back to the core concepts of retributive practices and restorative practices:

- **Retributive practices** describe a spectrum of tools that emphasize **compliance** as the context for community, **authority** as the response to conflict, and, when harm is created, **punishment** as the consequence.
- **Restorative practices** describe a spectrum of tools that emphasize **belonging** as the context for community, **connection** as the response to conflict, and, when harm is created, **reparation** as the consequence.

As you examine the cascade of misconceptions that lead school systems to promote a retributive approach over a restorative approach, begin to notice the ways in which these misconceptions may live in your own life, in your own relationships. This will serve you well in the next chapter on skills.

Chapter 2
Skill-Based Reasons

Student Outcomes Don't Change Until Adult Behaviors Change

There is a specific set of tools that a student-led approach to restorative practices seeks to teach about and then to teach proficiency with—tools that are as necessary for effective function in community as they are for the pursuit of maximization. Among those tools are self-regulation, metacognition, active listening, empathy, accountability, and responsibility. I have yet to visit with a teacher or parent who has suggested that these are tools they don't want their student to possess. And once these tools are developed, they open the door to the tools needed for restorative practices: belonging for community circles, connection for mediation circles, and reparation for restorative circles. All circles will be discussed in full in Part II.

But for adults to create the context in which students gain fluency with these tools, they must also be fluent with them, and they must be open to creating the conditions for students to routinely practice them. Often, neither of those is encouraged within school settings, in which case, student outcomes don't change until adult behaviors change. It is for that reason that our skill-building workshops, led by certified coaches and students who have already received training, are provided for both students and adults.

Insufficient Adult Training on Accountability and Responsibility

In Chapter 1, community is described as a group of people formed via a shared characteristic. Also discussed is that for students to experience maximization, they must have the ability to be in community effectively. That requires the students to be willing to make commitments and honor them. It also requires two-way commitments that, once entered into, are not easily discarded. We refer to these as agreements.

> **Commitment** describes what someone has allowed a person to expect.
>
> **Agreement** describes a shared commitment within a community.

Agreements are an essential aspect of community because they allow people within the community to know what to expect of each other. Such a sense of predictability allows communities to function. For example, when you accepted your driver's license, you entered into an agreement. Part of that agreement allows everyone else to expect that you'll stop at red lights while driving. This agreement radically increases the functioning of communities (simply imagine a city where no one stops at red lights to get my meaning).

Once agreements exist, the tools of accountability and responsibility exist. Both accountability and responsibility are crucial for maintaining a community. Unfortunately, those words are often used interchangeably even though they mean two very different things. Accountability is about identifying my agreements and determining whether they've been honored. Responsibility is about identifying how my behaviors are impacting my agreements. The terms are similar in form but entirely different in function.

In a school-based learning community, accountability and responsibility foster a sense of reliability and dependability, essentials for creating a positive and productive learning environment. When educators routinely demonstrate these tools, they set a powerful example for students and contribute to a community culture of trust and mutual respect.

Skill-Based Reasons

> **Accountability** describes the capacity to identify one's created agreements and the extent to which those agreements are honored or dishonored.
>
> **Responsibility** describes the capacity to identify one's created agreements and the ways in which behaviors are honoring or dishonoring those agreements.

Many schools do not provide training for educators on how to teach or foster accountability and responsibility among students. Traditional professional development appropriately tends to focus on curriculum and classroom management techniques rather than on strategies for developing fluency with those essential tools in students. Consequently, when conflicts arise, the response often focuses on immediate resolution through authority and the threat of punishment rather than on guiding students to understand their role in the situation and take responsibility for navigating it. That approach does not teach students the importance of accountability and responsibility, and it leads to superficial compliance instead of genuine understanding and growth.

Further, the lack of proper training on how to teach and foster accountability and responsibility can have significant negative consequences for both students and the school environment. Without the skills to use these tools, students may not develop a deep understanding of the importance of meeting commitments and taking responsibility for their actions, which can lead to a lack of trust and integrity within the school community.

For instance, students who are not taught accountability may repeatedly fail to meet deadlines or honor commitments, causing frustration for teachers and disrupting the learning environment. Similarly, when students are not guided to take responsibility for their actions, conflicts can escalate and become more difficult to navigate. When educators lack the training to foster these skills, they may struggle to create a positive and productive learning environment, which can result in decreased student engagement and increased behavioral issues, which can impact overall school performance.

Our Approach to Accountability and Responsibility

To develop the tools of accountability and responsibility, our approach to restorative practices teaches the Awareness / Acknowledgment / Aligned Action framework.

Awareness is about noticing what's going on in the world around you. Acknowledgment builds on your awareness by shifting your attention from what others are doing to noticing what you are doing that's contributing to what's going on in the world around you. Aligned Action builds on acknowledgment by inviting you to take a step in the direction of your intentions, grounded in full acknowledgment of your existing behaviors.

During our workshops, conversations often begin with awareness by asking questions like, "What are examples of times when people didn't honor their word at school?" This is an awareness question in that it invites participants to begin noticing patterns of behavior taking place in their school community.

The next question in the series then starts to push for acknowledgment: "Who will share a time when you didn't honor your word at school?" After the first couple of participants share, this question is fairly easy for the rest to step into. This is an acknowledgment question in that it transitions from noticing what others are doing to noticing what you're doing.

Awareness is absolutely necessary, but it is not by itself a path to either accountability or responsibility because it is always looking outward at what others are doing. Likewise, acknowledgment is absolutely necessary but also falls short of being a path to either accountability or responsibility. While acknowledgment does cause self-reflection, ideation alone is insufficient to generate accountability or responsibility. Only after action is taken that is aligned with acknowledgment is the space for accountability and responsibility created.

During our workshops, we practice these two steps—awareness and acknowledgment—over and over until participants are flawlessly capable of identifying both Awareness and Acknowledgment in their own lives in a variety of contexts. That is our way of testing whether participants have gained familiarity with the tool of accountability.

In student-led restorative practices, becoming thoroughly grounded in accountability is important because accountability is about the forest, not the trees; it's about the results of someone's agreements, not just their individual behavior. Someone proficient with the tool of accountability is likely to say:

Skill-Based Reasons

- "I admit when I have made a mistake and will take steps to correct it."
- "I consistently meet deadlines and fulfill my commitments."
- "I provide accurate and honest updates on my progress to those who rely on my work."

Once the participants have had a conversation that reveals accountability, the foundation for responsibility is laid. The next question in the sequence, once accountability is fully present, goes something like, "What is a step I can take in the direction of honoring my agreements?" The key word in that question is "step." It's about taking a step, not a leap. What is one tangible thing someone can do today or tomorrow that observably demonstrates that they're honoring their word—no matter how small of a step?

Getting participants to practice taking steps to honor their agreements moves them in the direction of being able to take actions that are aligned with their intentions. When participants can fully demonstrate acknowledgment and aligned action, this is our way of testing whether they have gained familiarity with the tool of Responsibility.

Responsibility is about the trees, not the forest; it's about individual behavior, not just the results of agreements. A participant proficient with the tool of responsibility is likely to say:

- "I completed my tasks on time without needing reminders."
- "I took responsibility for my mistakes and worked to correct them."
- "I followed through on agreements, even when it was difficult."

Insufficient Adult Training on Self-Regulation and Metacognition

As described in Chapter 1, homeostasis describes stability and regulation within one's environment. This is a key concept for understanding the benefits of self-regulation and metacognition.

Self-regulation describes the ability to feel triggered and still maintain homeostasis, and metacognition describes the ability to identify and regulate one's own thoughts. Both are critical tools on a student's path to maximization. They empower students to take control of their learning, cope with stress, and navigate complex social situations. When schools understand and promote these skills, they support students in building the resilience and autonomy necessary to experience maximization.

> **Self-regulation** describes the capacity for experiencing triggering circumstances while still managing thoughts, feelings, and behaviors—maintaining homeostasis.
>
> **Metacognition** describes the capacity for both awareness of what one is thinking and regulation of what one is thinking.

Unfortunately, many schools don't provide training for educators on how to teach or foster self-regulation and metacognition among students. Professional development often focuses on literacy and numeracy instruction—topics also essential to maximization—but omits equipping teachers with strategies to support students in developing the non-academic tools needed to fully leverage their academic tools. As a result, many educators may not feel confident or prepared to integrate self-regulation and metacognition tool development into their teaching practices.

The lack of training in fostering self-regulation and metacognition can have significant negative consequences for students and the overall school culture and climate. Without these tools, students may struggle to manage stress, maintain focus, and approach learning tasks strategically. That can result in increased behavioral issues, lower academic performance, and reduced engagement in school activities.

For instance, a student who lacks fluency with the tool of self-regulation may frequently disrupt the classroom, struggling to control their impulses or emotions. This behavior not only hinders their own learning but also impacts their peers and the learning community. Similarly, without metacognitive skills, students may have difficulty understanding their learning processes, which leads to poor study habits and lower educational attainment.

When school systems fail to have a plan to foster these tools, educators may feel ill equipped to support students in developing the necessary strategies for coping with challenges and succeeding academically and socially. Without that ability, educators may rely on traditional disciplinary measures that do not address the underlying issues, which perpetuates a cycle of frustration and disengagement.

Our Approach to Self-Regulation and Metacognition Training

To develop the tools of self-regulation and metacognition, the student-led approach to restorative practices teaches self-connection practice, which is adapted from Marshall Rosenburg's, non-violent communication work and book of the same name.

In self-connection practice, there are four steps:

1. Awareness: Observe Breath: First we invite participants to notice their own breathing by taking a deep breath. We invite them to get present with themselves and whatever they're experiencing in the moment, whether physical or emotional. Breathe in and out.
2. Acknowledgment: Identify Feelings: Next, we invite participants to identify and label the physical or emotional experience they're having in the moment. Are they feeling happy, sad, mad, glad, tired, thirsty, hot, cold, frustrated, or sore? Are they experiencing another physical or emotional feeling in the moment? The practice of noticing and being able to assign a label to one's internal environment is a major step in the direction of regulating that internal environment.

During our workshops, participants practice these two steps repeatedly. Being able to fully demonstrate both—Awareness: Observe Breath and Acknowledgment: Identify Feelings—is our way of testing for whether participants have gained familiarity with the tool of self-regulation. If so, we can add the next two steps.

In student-led restorative practices, self-regulation is about personal mastery, which is a major access to almost anything we want for ourselves in life. A participant who is proficient with the tool of self-regulation is likely to say:

"I can be present in moments when I am feeling upset."
"I can label how I'm feeling in the moment."
"I can control my impulses when I am tempted to act on them."

Once participants have demonstrated facility with the first two steps of self-connection practice, it's time for the third and fourth:

3. Acknowledgment: Identify Needs. This step is to identify and label what met and unmet need the feeling from the previous step might be pointing to.

- Examples when needs are not met:
    - "I'm feeling tired. I need a nap."
    - "I'm feeling thirsty. I need a drink."
    - "I'm feeling confused. I need understanding."
- Examples when needs are met:
    - "I'm feeling happy. My need for kindness has been met."
    - "I'm feeling grateful. My need for generosity has been met."

4. Aligned Action: Declare Commitment. Finally, in this step the participants identify a specific action that they could take in the moment that would take them in the direction of meeting the unmet need or honoring the met need. Again, any step—no matter how small—is still a step. A commitment in this context is a specific action that you allow yourself to expect of yourself. In keeping with the examples in number two above:

- Maybe you need calm, so you commit to taking a moment to breathe.
- Maybe you feel overwhelmed, so you commit to spending a few minutes on organizing the tasks and actions you need to take to reach your goals.
- Maybe you feel embarrassed after interrupting someone too many times, so you commit to controlling that impulse by learning to pause before speaking.

As participants in the workshops work through the process of self-connection practice, they get practice with being reflective about what's going on in their own minds and what they think would make a difference in their own lives. As participants demonstrate proficiency with Acknowledgment: Identify Needs and Aligned Action: Declare Commitment, we can verify whether they are growing in proficiency with the tool of metacognition.

In student-led restorative practices, metacognition is key for self-understanding and the decision-making skills that flow from it. A participant proficient with the tool of metacognition is likely to say:

- "I set specific goals before I begin a task."
- "I regularly ask myself if I am understanding what I'm observing or experiencing."
- "I change my strategies when I realize they are not working."

Insufficient Adult Training on Active Listening and Empathy

As first mentioned in Chapter 1, connection and conflict go hand in hand. Active listening and empathy are key elements of restoring connection. They foster a sense of communication and understanding, which are necessary for building strong relationships within a learning community. When educators practice and promote active listening and empathy, they create a more inclusive and supportive environment for students.

> **Active listening** describes the capacity to accurately hear what is said while accurately inferring what is meant.
>
> **Empathy** describes the capacity to identify with the feelings of others even when they do not match one's own.

That said, in general, schools don't provide training for teachers or principals on how to foster active listening and empathy among students. As mentioned previously, professional development often emphasizes required curriculum delivery and classroom discipline strategies rather than the interpersonal tools needed to build a compassionate and communicative school community. As a result, many educators may not feel equipped to effectively nurture these tools in their students. Instead, during a conflict between students, a teacher might focus on quickly resolving the issue themselves rather than helping the students listen to each other's perspectives, understand each other's feelings, and navigate the conflict themselves. Similarly, in daily interactions, opportunities to teach and model empathy might be overlooked in favor of an authoritative approach to maintaining order.

The lack of training in fostering active listening and empathy gives rise to significant unintended consequences for students and the overall learning environment. Without these tools, students may struggle to communicate effectively, navigate conflicts, and build meaningful relationships. This can lead to a lack of connection and understanding, which can decrease the likelihood of resilience in the face of educational challenges.

For instance, a student who does not practice active listening may frequently misunderstand instructions or fail to pick up on social cues, leading to frustration for both the student and their peers. Similarly, a lack of empathy can result in insensitive behavior, bullying, and an inability to work collaboratively with others.

When educators are not trained to foster these skills, they may miss opportunities to support students in developing the necessary interpersonal skills for navigating social situations effectively. That can lead to a classroom environment where students feel unheard and disconnected, which ultimately impacts their academic and social success.

Our Approach to Active Listening and Empathy Training

To nurture development of the tools of active listening and empathy, student-led restorative practices teaches interpersonal connection practice, which is also adapted from Marshall Rosenburg's work on nonviolent communication.

In interpersonal connection practice, there are four steps:

1. Awareness: Observe Participant: First, the participant observes what someone else says and reflects it back to them using the words of the speaker as an observation, not an interpretation, and their thoughts about what was said. It is absolutely vital that the participants practice observing rather than interpreting what is said. What that commonly sounds like is: "What I heard you say was…" or "When you said…"

> **Observation** describes what measurably happened.
>
> **Interpretation** describes a person's view of or the meaning they assign to what happened.

2. Acknowledgment: Identify Feelings: After participants have observed what was said, they guess at the physical or emotional experience the other person may be having in the moment. It's a guess, not a statement, because participants must acknowledge the reality that they don't actually know what someone else is feeling. That guess often sounds like: "Are you feeling…?" or "Did you mention feeling…?"

As with self-connection practice, interpersonal connection practice is practiced over and over during our workshops. Once participants have shown accuracy with these activities that have them focusing on someone else's reality—Awareness: Observe Participant and Acknowledgment: Identify

Skill-Based Reasons

Feelings—that suggests they have grown in proficiency with the tool of active listening.

In student-led restorative practices, active listening is a vital step on the path to empathy; without it, empathy is nearly impossible to achieve. Someone proficient with the tool of active listening is likely to say:

- "I make eye contact with the person I am speaking with and use body language to show I am listening."
- "I can repeat what the speaker has said to ensure I have understood correctly."
- "I ask questions to clarify a statement I may have misunderstood."

Once the first half of interpersonal connection practice is solid, then participants transition into working on the second half:

3. Acknowledgment: Identify Needs: In this step, the participants guess at what met or unmet need the speaker's feelings may be pointing to. Examples of how that often sounds include: "When you feel _____, are you needing...?" or "Do you have a need for...?" or "When you felt _____, was your need for _____ met/unmet?"
4. Aligned Action: Declare Agreement: After participants have surfaced the feelings and needs, they create agreements that everyone is willing to agree to regarding what each person is willing to do to either address the unmet need or honor the met need. Participants end up saying things like, "To meet our need for peace, we're going to walk away when we're feeling frustrated," or "To honor your need for support, I'm going to ask if you need support so we can talk when you seem frustrated."

This intentional practicing of interpersonal connection grows the participants' ability to better understand not only their own needs but the needs of those around them. We often refer to this as "getting out of our own world and into someone else's world" when we go out of our way to understand what's real for them. When participants can effectively get into someone else's world through these two steps—Acknowledgment: Identify Needs and Aligned Action: Declare Agreements—they are indicating whether they are competent with the tool of empathy.

In student-led restorative practices, empathy is key to unlocking connection, which is key to navigating conflict. A participant who has demonstrated proficiency with the tool of empathy is likely to say things like:

- "I can easily understand how someone else feels even if I haven't been in their situation."
- "I feel concern for people even when they are different from me."
- "I try to look at everyone's side of a disagreement before I make a decision."

Belonging, Connection, and Reparation

When students aren't provided with the basic tool development described above, they are likely to lack the ability to create or experience belonging, connection, and reparation in their communities.

Because belonging describes how we feel perceived by others, and is often experienced as acceptance and inclusion within a community, self-regulation and metacognition are necessary. Without the abilities to manage ourselves and reflect on our own thinking, all we can reasonably hope for as the context for community is compliance that is externally enforced. This is why we use community circles as the instrument for teaching belonging and why we use effectiveness at facilitating community circles as the measure of proficiency with belonging. Instead of merely being resigned to compliance, a student proficient with the practice of belonging is likely to say:

- "I feel like I am a valued member of my group or community."
- "I have strong relationships with the people around me."
- "I feel included in activities and discussions."

Because connection describes how we feel about others and is often experienced as an emotional bond with individuals within a community, active listening and empathy are necessary. Without the abilities to infer someone else's meaning and recognize their experiences that give rise to it, all we can reasonably hope for in response to conflict is to rely on external authority to demand of us what our skills don't allow us to achieve for ourselves. This is why we use mediation circles as the instrument for teaching connection and why we use effectiveness at facilitating mediation circles as the measure of proficiency with connection. Instead of waiting for someone with authority to come along, a student proficient with the practice of connection is likely to say:

- "I have deep and meaningful conversations with the people in my life."
- "I feel close to and connected with my family and friends."
- "I can share my thoughts and feelings openly with others."

Skill-Based Reasons

Because reparation describes healing the harm created and often is experienced as harm being healed within the context of a community, accountability and responsibility are necessary. Without the abilities to be clear about our agreements, whether we are honoring them, and what the result of dishonoring them is causing, the best option remaining to us when harm occurs is often punishment. This is why we use restorative circles as the instrument for teaching reparation and why we use effectiveness at facilitating restorative circles as the measure of proficiency with reparation. Instead of being victims of circumstance and hoping that punishment magically solves everything, students proficient with the practice of reparation are likely to say:

- "I take responsibility and take action when I have hurt someone."
- "I actively work to address harm I've created and restore our community."
- "I seek to understand how I failed to meet expectations and improve."

Our Tools

In summary, adults likely have certain tools but likely have not been supported in how best to cultivate the same tools in their students. Fortunately, there are specific practices that can support the cultivation within our students of the tools they deserve. But first we have to support the adults to do so, and then we must create a great deal of opportunity for students to practice so that they become proficient.

Because this is exceedingly rare, in the absence of these tools, adults rely on retribution.

A Student-Led Approach to Restorative Practices Uses These Basic Practices	Those Practices Cultivate These Tools
Self-Connection Practice	
1. Awareness: Observe Breathing	Self-Regulation
2. Acknowledgment: Identify Feelings	
3. Acknowledgment: Identify Needs	Metacognition
4. Aligned Action: Declare Commitment	
Interpersonal Connection Practice	
1. Awareness: Observe Participant	Active Listening
2. Acknowledgment: Identify Feelings	
3. Acknowledgment: Identify Needs	Empathy
4. Aligned Action: Declare Commitment	
Awareness/Acknowledgment/Aligned Action	
1. Awareness	Accountability
2. Acknowledgment	
3. Aligned Action	Responsibility

Skill-Based Reasons

These Tools Enable These Restorative Practices	Those Practices Cultivate These Tools	Withouth These Tools, Adults Rely On
Community Circles	Belonging	Compliance instead of Belonging
Mediation Circles	Connection	Authority instead of Connection
Restorative Circles	Reparation	Punishment instead of Reparation

Chapter 3
Mindset-Based Reasons

The Societal Agreement and Adultism

Adults almost never intend to be harmful to children. Across human society, there is a societal-level agreement regarding children: adults have a duty to care for them. Because of this ingrained societal agreement, most adults go out of their way to protect children, even if they don't know them. This is a wonderful aspect of our society.

Inherent in that duty to care is the healthy and beautiful obligation to set boundaries when the absence of boundaries could cause harm for the child. If a child wants to play in traffic, we set boundaries to prevent that because of the harm it could cause. If a child wants to eat only ice cream three times per day, we set boundaries to prevent that because of the harm it could cause. Despite such positive protective outcomes, it is also inescapable that this societal agreement results in a massive reduction in the autonomy that children experience. We accept this trade-off in exchange for children successfully growing up.

At its core, many aspects of our public education system—with spending nationwide that is nearly what we spend on defense—and our other safety-net programs for children are born out of the societal agreement about children. All of this—the institutions, the boundary setting, etc.—speak to the adult inclination toward protecting the well-being of children. When you begin to reflect on the expansiveness and near universality of the societal agreement about children, it's quite astounding.

But if this agreement is so powerful, why do so many children live in suffering and without access to the tools they need? Unfortunately, even though we subscribe to this grand agreement, our view of the world can be in powerful contradiction to what the societal agreement about children implies. Collectively, school systems are often trapped inside ways of seeing the world that hide the truth: many of our schools are in active violation of the societal agreement. Until we challenge our hidden but very present views of the world—until we challenge our mindset about schooling—this violation regarding children will remain.

It is not by accident that most school systems trend toward adult-led retribution rather than student-led restoration. It's a matter of mindset. Absent having student maximization as a core mindset, an adult-led mindset with a retribution-focused lens prevails. From that perspective, adult leadership is the best option regardless of the impact on children, and retribution is the best option regardless of the impact on children. However, that mindset inevitably gives rise to systems that contribute to the minimization of students.

This mindset is a subtle form of adultism—a way of viewing the world that justifies oppressive behavior targeted at people who are not adults for the benefit of those who are adults. Like all oppression, the damage to the oppressed has the capacity to create significant and lasting harm. Adultism is a perversion of the societal agreement about children.

To be perfectly clear, adult behavior that honors the societal agreement to care for children is not adultism, even when the child doesn't appreciate the boundaries. Just because a child doesn't like an adult's decision doesn't make it adultist. But when adult behavior takes advantage of the societal agreement and uses the power it confers for adult benefit, convenience, or comfort, that is adultism. The apartheid nature of schools—that there are more students than adults but that the adults have all ultimate authority—is sometimes a necessity of the societal agreement about children. Any abuses of the apartheid nature of schools for adult benefit, convenience, comfort is not.

While the worldviews of adult leadership and retribution might seem completely reasonable at first glance, a deeper examination highlights ways that they can be abused in ways that are both misleading and openly harmful. This chapter addresses several claims I routinely hear in schools that are at odds with student maximization and that reveal adultist mindset-based reasons student-led restorative practices are not used.

"Behavior Is Best Addressed Through Punishment"

One mindset that leads to violations of the societal agreement about children is that the optimal way to educate children to make good behavior choices is by punishing unwanted behaviors in a harsh enough manner that it encourages desired behavior choices. That belief seemed worth testing, so in one school system, we had student discipline data analyzed for a five-year period. The school system had a four-tier discipline system. It's reductive, but an example of the tiers was essentially:

- Tier 1: A child yelled at someone.
- Tier 2: A child pushed someone.
- Tier 3: A child punched someone.
- Tier 4: A child hit someone with a weapon.

What we found was that over the five-year period, there were almost no examples of tier 4 infractions that weren't preceded by tier 2 or tier 3 infractions, and there weren't many tier 3 infractions that weren't preceded by tier 1 or tier 2 infractions.

Our takeaway from this analysis was pretty simple: if you address behavior in an effective manner at the tier 1 level, it can have the result of decreasing tier 4 infractions. Nothing in the analysis, however, in any way suggested that retributive approaches to tier 1 infractions decreased the likelihood of tier 2, tier 3, or tier 4 infractions. Behavior is a form of communication, and our students are communicating things to us at an early enough level that often, if we understand them, we can try to figure out what we can do. If there are situations that we can engage with at the tier 1 level, we can often prevent things from escalating to a tier 4 level.

Instead of taking that approach, however, another manifestation of the adultist mindset is the belief that punishment is the most effective avenue for justice. This view holds that improving student outcomes when children misbehave is best accomplished through punishment, with the idea that sufficiently harsh penalties will deter future misbehavior and maintain order. There is some evidence that if the punishment is harsh enough and swift enough, it can serve as a deterrent. But that evidence doesn't suggest an increase in character development or an improvement in student outcomes; these simply aren't the focus of punishment. Instead, this is often what it looks like in practice.

Restorative Approach to Justice	Retributive Approach to Justice
Can be more long-term time efficient; generally takes more time upfront	Often more near-term time efficient; generally takes less time upfront
More maximization oriented	Less maximization oriented
Violation of norms, agreements, and rules defined as harm requiring repair	Violation of norms, agreements, and rules defined as harm requiring punishment
Focuses on being responsible and repairing the harm	Focuses on establishing guilt and punishing the guilty
Focuses on relationships and student outcomes	Focuses on rules and adult inputs
Conflict represented as opportunity for learning	Conflict represented as something to prevent
Community included in process	Community excluded from process

Mindset-Based Reasons

Restorative Approach to Justice	Retributive Approach to Justice
Relies on choice	Relies on force
Accountability defined as acknowledging the harm created, taking responsibility for choices, and working to repair the harm	Accountability defined as being appropriately punished—experiencing harm in equal measure to the harm created
Intentionally attempts to avoid violence	May unintentionally perpetuate violence
Will not be universally effective; there are specific conditions in which a restorative approach contributes to justice	Will not be universally effective; there are specific conditions in which a retributive approach contributes to justice

Challenging this adultist mindset is crucial mostly because that mindset doesn't work to inspire maximization. While punishment provides immediate consequences—and student-led restorative practices are *strongly* pro-consequences—it often fails to address underlying causes and can lead to negative long-term outcomes. A restorative approach supports students with understanding the impact of their actions, taking accountability for their actions, and developing the tools necessary for maximization.

Please do not misunderstand: a student-led approach to restorative practices is not in opposition to using retributive approaches in schools in some cases. However, an overreliance on retribution or a reliance on retribution as the primary response to behavior isn't well evidenced if the intention is maximization for the student being punished. Further, it benefits adults more than children and can cause harm without justification.

"If I Can't Have It..."

Our recommendation is for all adults in the school, regardless of role, to go through training on this work. Evidence of why that is a good idea came during one of our orientation workshops in which some of the school system's security officers were present. Having their insights throughout the workshop provided a very different perspective to the rest of the participants.

At the end of the multi-day workshop, we often go around the circle and invite closing comments. One of the officers who hadn't spoken much raised his hand to speak. "I've been with this district for a long time," he said, "and this is the first time I've ever been invited to participate in a training alongside teachers. It's like we don't matter all day long until something bad happens, and then everyone wants us to swoop in and fix it. We are treated like second-class employees compared to teachers."

You could have heard a pin drop. He hadn't spoken with an angry voice, just the earnest timbre of a man who had held in his truth for a long time and had finally been given the chance to share it.

After a few moments of silence, one of the teacher leaders motioned to speak next. "I had no idea," she said, "but now that you've said it, that makes perfect sense. I look for ways to collaborate with other teachers. I've not looked for that with our safety team."

It may sound odd, but for student-led restorative practices to have a meaningful chance of being implemented faithfully in a school, every adult in the building needs to be trained and needs to be treated as a partner in the work. That means every adult co-creates a restorative culture, but it also means every adult deserves to experience a restorative culture.

If adults don't have access to restoration, and if they aren't included in its creation, don't expect them to consistently or sustainably provide it to students. Adults are unlikely to give what they themselves are not getting. When adults are subjected to a retributive system, it's inevitable that this is the system they'll reproduce for their students. Said differently, better learning conditions for students typically require better working conditions for adults.

While I strongly empathize with that need, it's nevertheless unacceptable to wait until every adult is getting what they need. Even while adults struggle to get working conditions that allow them to be the best versions of themselves in schools, we remain obligated to provide students with the best opportunities we can.

"Students Want to Violate Agreements"

When we are getting student leaders prepared to take more responsibility for leading student trainings, a large part of their preparation is practice with self-regulation in the face of frustration. Few people get frustrated with teenage behavior as quickly as teenagers themselves who are accountable for their peers' behavior.

Mindset-Based Reasons

One of our student leaders, a highly extroverted sophomore, struggled with impulsivity in the face of noncompliant peer behavior. It wasn't that he didn't have great leadership instincts; it was just that by the time he was in a place to deploy them, he'd already said or done something that made it hard for him to be an effective leader. When I talked to him about it the first time, he blew up at me and then stormed off. A teacher standing next to me was disturbed by his behavior and didn't understand why I was so calm about it.

"He'll be back," I said simply and then went about my tasks.

Sure enough, he eventually returned and apologized for blowing up. We talked through it and discussed some strategies he could use going forward, and then he went right back to being the leader I knew he could be. Much of the self-regulatory training that is included in student-led restorative practices focuses on students being able to notice when they are triggered and using the practices we teach to de-escalate themselves. This is exactly what he was doing. He just wasn't proficient at it yet.

Over time, this same pattern played out in similar fashion, but with de-escalating amounts of energy and decreasing amounts of time between when he would go off and when he would come back. The last time it happened, the same teacher was there who witnessed the first time. "Wow, he doesn't get frustrated nearly as much or for nearly as long anymore," the teacher exclaimed.

That's what the work looks like. In math class, we have to choose how to manage the reality that students aren't yet good at math—but with their hard work and our support, they'll get there. Similarly, in "behavior class"—which is to say, all of life—we will have to choose how to manage the reality that students sometimes aren't yet good at self-regulation. But with their hard work and our support, they'll get there.

The adultist mindset often assumes that students inherently want to violate rules and expectations set by adults rather than considering that often students are simply still learning to use the tools at their disposal. This mindset views students as naturally rebellious and disruptive, which is convenient in that it alleviates adults of the responsibility for managing our own responses to students who are still in a place of learning.

"We Must Protect the Kids Who Want to Learn From the Kids Who Don't"

At its core, the adultist world view holds that many students are inherently disruptive and disinterested in learning, which threatens the educational opportunities of the "good" students who are motivated and eager to learn. This retributive focus justifies strict disciplinary measures to separate the "good" students from the "bad" ones, aiming to protect the learning environment for those deemed deserving.

Thus, in many schools, this adultist mindset leads to policies and practices that seek to swiftly and severely eliminate disruptive behavior by permanently removing those perceived as threats. However, this mindset overlooks that those students want to succeed as well. When students misbehave, once the learning environment is protected, a student-led approach to restorative practices invites curiosity. We ask, "What tools is this student missing that would change their behavior? What would be possible if the focus was on supporting the student with acquiring those tools?"

For example, if a student fails a math quiz, we don't suspend them for five days with the belief that doing so will magically cause them to learn math. Instead, we make them aware of how they performed – we don't pretend they didn't fail the quiz, but we don't demonize it either—and we invite them to acknowledge that with their hard work and our support, they can and will improve. We reteach the math they are missing. Then we give them an opportunity to act on what they've learned: we give them the math quiz again.

What a retributive mindset about behavior is missing is that we can apply this exact same approach when students "fail" the "behavior quiz" that is day-to-day life in a school. When a student fails the behavior quiz, we must make them aware that their behavior was not acceptable. But we must also invite them to acknowledge that with their hard work and our support, they can and will improve. We reteach the tools they are missing. Then we give them an opportunity to act on what they've learned: we give them the behavior quiz again.

What the retributive approach would have us believe is that when a student fails the behavior quiz, sending them home for five days will cause them to pause in contrite meditation during that time and reflect on how best to improve their behavior. Anyone who has ever worked with students knows that this is largely nonsense. More likely, the student will spend the time playing games and sending text messages to students who are at school.

Mindset-Based Reasons

We can do better.

Part II
How Students Can Practice Restoration

Step One: Focus Mindset

Chapter 4
Maximization

Minimization

As we were preparing to begin a multiday workshop to train a new group of middle schoolers, one of the school's staff shared a concern with a colleague. Seeing one of the students, Monica, arrive at the workshop space, she said, "Monica is one of the worst-behaved students in the school. Why are we rewarding her by letting her be one of the peer leaders?"

We hear questions like this regularly. They simultaneously come from a supportive place—wanting to ensure that the workshop goes well—and a retributive place—wanting a student who has behaved poorly to be punished by being removed from what is seen as a privilege. They highlight what is often missed about the intention of student-led restorative practices. That is, students can be relied upon to use the most appropriate tool in their toolbox to address whatever circumstances they face. If you experience a student trying to hammer a screw, the first question to ask is whether they have a screwdriver instead of assuming that they have one and simply are choosing to use an inappropriate tool.

What became of Monica, the "worst-behaved" student? Perhaps not surprisingly, she went on to become one of our more impressive student leaders. She became co-captain of the basketball team—both because she got her grades up enough to be eligible and because her coaches now considered her a role model. There was never really a question of whether Monica was a leader; other students were already following her. The only real question was where she would choose to lead them. The answer—pretty much as always—was that she would lead in whatever direction the tools at her disposal inspired her to lead. As we supported her in adding more tools to her toolbox, she became capable of leading in new ways.

But what if we had followed the staffer's guidance? What if we had denied Monica the opportunity to participate because her behavior required a punitive consequence? Regardless of our good intentions, by choosing to ban her from the program, we would have been engaging a minimization mindset. To understand maximization fully, you need to understand minimization.

Where a maximization mindset is about supporting students to experience the fullness of their possibility, a minimization mindset is about constraining them. And while that concept already seems disturbing enough, it actually gets worse. Even when we don't initially see it, whenever minimization occurs, there is a benefit to the minimizer. For example, if Monica's teacher had succeeded in having Monica banned from the activity, the teacher would have proven to Monica who had the power in the room, and the teacher would have gotten to avoid being around Monica and any disruptions she may have caused over the next few days. We must always remain aware of the potential built-in benefits for the minimizer because they are constantly whispering in the back of our minds and inspiring minimizing choices that we might otherwise not make, often without us noticing.

> **Maximization** describes both the extent to which a person experiences the optimal possibility their circumstances allow and the expansion of those circumstances for all persons.
>
> **Minimization** describes both the extent to which a person experiences being contained to what benefits those doing the containing and the expansion of that containment to more persons.

Again, the result of maximization is that people experience the maximal expression of who they are capable of being as growing, sentient, sapient individuals such that they can live choice-filled lives on their own terms, able to care for themselves, their loved ones, and their communities. Maximization creates the experience of choice.

The result of minimization is that people experience the minimal expression of who they are capable of being. Their growth and their experience of sentience and sapience as individuals is stunted, and they experience fewer choices with which to live life on their own terms and care for themselves, their loved ones, and their communities. Minimization creates the experience of control.

While it is important to be clear that the staff member at Monica's school did want the workshop to go well, it's equally important to be clear that her question was also about retribution for Monica's past behaviors. By acknowledging that, it becomes clear that retribution is an agent of minimization. Again, this does not mean that retribution is bad or wrong, but it does cause the expansion of minimization. If that is what we want for our schools, this is not problematic at all. But if maximization is what we want for our schools, we need to be mindful about how and when we deploy strategies that undermine it. Sometimes we will choose to do so as a hyper-protective approach to ensure the health and well-being of our other students. For example, if you bring a loaded weapon into my school, I will deploy a retributive strategy—likely suspension or expulsion. And I will do this with a clear conscience knowing full well that it will produce an increase of minimization in your life. But that example is at the extreme margins of behavior. Of the tens of millions of students going to school every day, only a handful arrive with loaded weapons.

So why would retribution and minimization be the ideas around which we design our default behaviors? Unfortunately, often the real answer to this question is "That's what we've always done."

Presenced and Patterned

Have you ever been driving home from work or school and arrived in front of your home, and then suddenly you realize you have absolutely no recollection of the drive? It's actually kind of remarkable when you think about it: you successfully maneuvered an incredibly heavy, fast-moving machine across a distance that might take hours to walk, all while turning, slowing down, and speeding up, and you have no memory of the journey!

In those moments when you aren't present to your driving, consider that there are benefits and costs of not being present. Most often the benefits were that you got to reflect on your day, wind down, or just listen to a favorite podcast or playlist—free from the anxiety of dealing with travel or all the other drivers on the road. Then there are costs, from the obvious, like potential safety costs of not being present to the road, to the less obvious cost of missing out on seeing something beautiful or forgetting to stop for groceries on your way home.

This example highlights two overarching ways of living in the moment: being present—fully alive, fully awake, fully available in the moment so that your choices create the future—or being patterned, where whatever you have repeatedly done before simply gets repeated again, and your past creates the future. While driving your car when you are not present in the moment, you are doing so based on the patterns of behavior you have created over time. Patterns by themselves are neither good nor bad; they are simply patterns, much like breathing. When you stop being present to your breathing, what happens? You don't die; instead, the pattern for breathing asserts itself.

> **Presenced** describes when you are fully available in the moment such that your choices create the future.
>
> **Patterned** describes when you are unavailable in the moment such that previous reactions to triggers repeat themselves and create the future.

I'm particularly grateful for the pattern of breathing. I certainly prefer it to the alternative. But what's worth exploring is that in the moment when I am being patterned in my breathing rather than being present to my breathing, the pattern is running the show. Conversely, in the moments when I am fully present to my breathing, I get to choose the future for breathing. I can take deep breaths. Shallow breaths. Hold my breath entirely. In the moments when I am patterned to breathing, the patterns create the future. In the moments when I am present to breathing, my choices create the future.

The intersection where being presenced and patterned meet is the reality maximization confronts: it is entirely possible to wake up in the driveway of our patterned lives ten, twenty, fifty years from now and have no recollection of the journey. Having never experienced or caused maximization. Having simply reproduced the way we've always done things.

If the pattern of our life today is maximization, then this might be welcome news. But as you begin to get present to the patterns in your life—not merely in driving but also in relationships, in your work, in your faith, in your family, in your friendships—and as you reflect on the Monicas in your life, notice the areas where the patterned way of being is not creating maximization.

In those moments—when our patterned way of being is not creating the future we want—presence is necessary. Presenced isn't good or bad. But if you want to create something new, patterns will not do; patterns will only take you where they've always taken you. Going someplace new requires presence. Presence is a prerequisite of maximization.

Survival Priority

As we begin to get present to the pattern of minimization in our schools and in our own lives, an even more dominant pattern comes into view: survival priority.

Throughout this book, I repeatedly recommend a policy bias toward strategies that are more likely to support maximization. A significant reason for this recommendation is that it serves as a counter for a dominant pattern that many schools face. The less someone's personal focus is on maximization in their life, the more they focus on survival—whether real (observed) or perceived (interpreted), whether physical, social, or psychological. In other words, when students are not supported on the path to maximization, their biology's default and dominant pattern, their survival priority, surges forward. Schools where students are focused on their own maximization, in whatever form that takes, are very different places than schools where large parts of the student body are operating from a place of survival priority.

Have you ever seen a student who is so scared or angry that it seems as if they can't even see you, let alone communicate with you? As if no one is home inside? If so, then you've seen the extreme of being overtaken by full-on survival priority. And while in such extreme throes of survival priority, humans—whether individually or collectively—are never fully capable of experiencing or expressing maximization. They don't just seem as if they can't communicate; they truly can't.

The less time students spend pursuing and experiencing maximization, the more likely they are to retreat to a survival priority mindset where the immediate goal is to avoid stress and discomfort. Because of that, survival priority often prevents students from accessing the higher-order thinking and emotional regulation needed for maximization. When stuck in survival priority mode, they are unable to engage fully in the learning process or in their own development. In contrast, maximization nurtures a mindset of possibility, where students can see beyond their current circumstances and envision a future of their own design.

As humans, we are born into survival priority as the default pattern. We are molded, nurtured, and informed by it until we reach a level of maturity and self-awareness that allows us to step outside of its constant grasp. These patterns become ingrained over time, and without new tools, we repeat them again and again. Eventually, they become the only responses we know, which creates our futures based on the pattern of survival priority.

As with every topic in this book, survival priority is neither good nor bad, right nor wrong. Like breathing, it can be a vitally important pattern in the moments when it is needed. It's just that survival priority is only focused on survival; it's not a pattern that will take us toward experiencing the fullness of our potential. This phenomenon goes beyond the individual student; it applies at the level of society as well because the well-being of any society hinges on the well-being of the children in that society. When a society's children experience their full potential, the society as a whole has greater access to its collective potential. I suspect we all have an inherent sense of this interconnectedness, hence the societal agreement about children.

A key argument for why education exists at the societal level is that it serves as a bulwark against society being trapped in survival priority and instead engaging in the pursuit of maximization. As a thing we choose to do in society, education has the potential to generate maximization for students, which allows our collective potential to be revealed. The reason societies choose to invest such a phenomenal amount of resources into education for children is to create a pathway toward our collective maximization.

On an individual basis, however, it can be challenging to figure out how best to actualize this pathway. Anyone who has spent any time working in schools knows that it is incredibly challenging work. Creating the space for maximization of all students in a school system requires tremendous effort. Instead of fighting for that, it appears that our education system—at both a macro and micro level—often lowers the bar and embraces an ethos of maximization for the "good kids," or the educationally privileged kids, and a very low floor of expectation for everyone else. Focusing only on fluency with literacy and numeracy tools without also ensuring that students have fluency with necessary tools such as responsibility, accountability, empathy, active listening, metacognition, and self-regulation is accepting a low expectation for what our education system can do. The ideal is that children gain literacy at home, but if that doesn't happen, schools must ensure that students have this tool. Similarly, the ideal is that children gain accountability at home, but if that doesn't happen, schools must ensure that students have that tool too. The reductive approach to what we expect from our education systems is fueled by policy decisions at the national/federal level, the state/regional level, and even the local/individual level.

Inside these low expectations, it's entirely acceptable that some students have access to maximization and other students are left to the ravages of runaway survival priority. There is no expectation that our strategies must align

Maximization

with what would be necessary to create the conditions for maximization of all students. Divorced from a maximization mindset for our education system, retribution as a strategy isn't merely inevitable; it's preferable since we'd need a way to manage the students who "aren't interested in" or "aren't ready for" maximization. In these moments, it can be easy for school system leaders to feel as if the highly regulated environment of schooling forces them into focusing on being compliant to the rules of distant funding and accrediting bodies. Then, as education systems increasingly see their reason for existing as being compliant to the rules of distant authority figures—and as they become convinced of horrific punishments that will befall them if they fall out of line—compliance, authority, and punishment become desirable allies for adults. Once this happens, of course, compliance, authority, and punishment become seen as reasonable strategies for students as well.

- **Retributive practices** describe a spectrum of tools that emphasize **compliance** as the context for community, **authority** as the response to conflict, and, when harm is created, **punishment** as the consequence.

Only inside a maximization mindset does the societal cost and challenge associated with restoration as a strategy toward maximization become worthy of investment. Only in that context do belonging, connection, and reparation make enough sense to be worth investing in.

- **Restorative practices** describe a spectrum of tools that emphasize **belonging** as the context for community, **connection** as the response to conflict, and, when harm is created, **reparation** as the consequence.

Investing in a path toward maximization invites people to live a life of meaning—to be a contribution to something larger than yourself. The benefits of student-led restorative practices as a pathway to maximization go beyond the knowledge of and skill with the tools we teach about. Few things in life open us to our own journey toward our potential like contributing to something greater than ourselves. As Monica stepped into being a leader in new ways, not only did she add to her tool box but she experienced herself and what she had to offer the world in a new way. Having access to new tools is like suddenly having a spotlight turned on. We see things in a new light, see things we never saw possible before, and a new path opens up to get us where we want to go.

Monica's teacher was not a bad person; I happen to know she's a teacher I'd be excited to have for my own children. But her greatness is muted by an education system that sometimes accepts the minimization of children as the standard operating procedure. This chapter is not about good and bad or right and wrong. It is about the desired educational results we want for our children. If we don't identify and address our minimization-oriented practices dominating our schools, and if we don't identify and address where survival priority is the pattern dominating our behaviors, there will be larger implications. The well-being of our society is placed at risk if we do not rethink our approach to education. A maximization mindset is vital.

Chapter 5
Trust

Speed of Trust

In all the years that I have done this work, I have never once seen a student-led restorative practices initiative fall apart because of students. Invariably when they implode, they do so because of adults. But more specifically than that, they do so because adults choose not to honor their agreements.

Part of what we do to lay the foundation to deploy student-led restorative practices is provide a two-day orientation workshop. The intention is for every single adult in the school—all of them, without exception—to go through the workshop. Because adults not honoring their agreements is such a powerful hindrance to students getting the tools they deserve, one of the very first invitations to self-reflection we have during the workshop presses this issue. The inquiry is direct:

> *What was a time when my behavior made it*
> *harder for children/students to trust?*

As you consider this question, begin to reflect on your own life and the times when your choices, your adult behaviors, may not have honored the agreements you allowed young people to expect of you. Maybe you said you would help with something, and you did not. Or maybe you allowed children to expect that you would listen to them, and you did not. Maybe you agreed to do something they wanted to do, but ultimately you did not do it. Begin to notice the moments when you allowed young people to have expectations of you that you did not honor.

During the workshop, this is often the moment when participants begin to identify the various reasons that they did not honor their agreements. They often formulate arguments suggesting they didn't have a choice in whether to honor their word. Our coaches, however, have been trained for this moment and are neither bothered by these efforts nor deterred by them—the arguments are, unfortunately, quite common, so we're prepared for them. Instead, our commitment is to support adults at looking, without judgment but also without pretending, at the moments when we have chosen not to honor our agreements with children.

In the moments when we choose not to honor our agreements, our word is like a bicycle wheel that is missing its spokes: it lacks structural integrity. As a result, we create for ourselves less access to our intentions. If our intention is to generate a trusting relationship with our students, in the moment we choose not to honor our agreements, our word lacks integrity, and our intention—trust and relationship—becomes harder to access. The bicycle wheel without spokes lacks structural integrity and will make it harder to access the intention of riding the bicycle. When our word lacks structural integrity because we choose not to honor our agreements, it becomes harder for us to access our intentions.

Notice that the question to our participants is not *if* there are moments when their behavior made it harder for children to trust adults because they didn't honor their agreements. Whether or not they have behaved in ways that have made it harder for children to trust is not in question. What *is* in question, however, is whether they are willing to acknowledge the moments when what they have allowed young people to expect and what they have done are incongruent. When we are willing to confront this reality in our choices, our ability to access our intentions increases. This is what is meant by the speed of trust. When trust is present between students and adults, we can access our intentions more quickly. But when we are unwilling to confront this reality—when instead we indulge in the comfortable practice of pretending—what's possible for our students becomes a little less and a little less.

Once more, this is not a conversation about good or bad or right or wrong. Such judgments are neither productive for nor germane to our intention. It's a conversation about noticing the relationship between our word and our access to the goals we intend.

Analysis

Once participants have wrestled with this question, we deepen the conversation. It's not enough to notice our behavior that may have made it harder for students to trust. It's essential that we inquire more deeply into what was going on with us in the moments we chose to behave that way. To access these insights, participants answer this question:

> *In the moment when I chose to behave in a manner that may have made it harder for students to trust, what was the benefit to me?*

Notice again that the question is not *if* there is a benefit. There is definitely a benefit. The task is to identify it. Children are harmed when adults indulge in pretending—pretending that we haven't behaved in this manner and further pretending that there wasn't a benefit for us to do so. The more open we are to authentically reflecting on our own behavior, the more powerful of an ally we can be to our students.

Maybe the benefit was convenience—honoring our word would have been inconvenient, so we didn't. Or maybe the benefit was avoidance—honoring our word would have brought us into conflict with adults. Or maybe the benefit was time—honoring our word would have taken time away from other things that we'd rather do. In our sessions with adults, convenience, conflict avoidance, and time are among the most common benefits that inspire us to behave in ways that undermine our students' ability to trust us.

As you might imagine, this second question can lead into an even less comfortable conversation than the first one. But our commitment is to the greatness of our students, not to the comfort of the adults. We don't seek out adult discomfort, but we also don't avoid it just to benefit adults at the expense of children. The more fully that we as adults get present to both our behavior that's making it harder for students to be successful and the circumstances that seduced us into that behavior, the greater the likelihood that we will make new choices that create a new future for ourselves and our students.

Only after participants in the workshop have effectively wrestled with both the behavior and the benefit do we move to the next step in the conversation: the cost. In every moment that there is a benefit to someone by behaving in a particular way, there is a cost to the students they serve. The next question uncovers what that cost is.

> *In the moment I chose to behave that way and received a benefit, what was the cost to students? What cost did students pay so that I could enjoy the benefit I gained?*

It's in these moments that workshop participants connect the dots between what they have been doing and what students have been experiencing. This conversation begins to reveal the extent to which a gap exists between our intentions and our impact. The more open we are to engaging in this conversation, as difficult as it may be, the greater the likelihood that we can be the people we intend to be in the lives of the young people around us.

But even as challenging as this conversation can be, there is one more aspect that we invite participants into. Because it's not enough to reflect on our behavior, the benefits to us from behaving that way, and the cost to students when we choose to do so. To really open ourselves up to a shift in mindset that leads away from damaging students' ability to trust adults, we need to confront the stories we've been telling ourselves and others.

Pretending

In the story of my life, there's a clear good guy: me. The same can be said for you reading this and everyone else. But in the moments when our behavior isn't honoring our beliefs, values, and commitments and, instead, is making it harder for students to trust, we need to make a choice. We can acknowledge the behavior we engaged in that made it harder for students to trust adults and, through so doing, begin to replace the spokes in the wheel of our leadership. Or we can 1) create a story, a way of justifying our behavior that allows us to no longer appear responsible for having created the distrust that now exists, and then 2) refuse to accept that we created the story but instead treat it like an external reality of which we're merely observers or victims. When we choose to behave this way instead, this is referred to as pretending. Pretending is so powerful because we create something and then act as if we didn't create it.

Once participants have gotten fully present to the behavior, the benefit, and the cost, it's time for the next layer: the pretending.

> *In the moment I chose to behave in a way that*
> *made it harder for students to trust, what was*
> *I pretending?*

Here, participants sit with the question for a moment and begin to notice the stories they've created that they haven't taken responsibility for creating. That is, stories that help to provide a reason or a justification for our behavior. Again, none of this is about good, bad, right, or wrong. It's about noticing what is at play in our choices, our adult behaviors. It's common that participants share things like:

- "I was pretending that the students wouldn't notice."
- "I was pretending that my time was more important than my students' time."
- "I was pretending that it didn't matter."
- "I was pretending that they misunderstood what I meant."
- "I was pretending that I was too busy when really I was just too tired."
- "I was pretending that it was their fault or another adult's fault."

Whatever the pretending is, we begin to identify it for the purpose it serves, which is to preserve our role as the good guy in the story of our lives. But also we begin to identify the cost of clinging to the pretending: we give away parts of our power to be transformative in the lives of the students we say that we're committed to.

Openings

As we get fully present to our behaviors that make it harder for students to trust, our benefits, the costs to the students, and our pretending, we fully open the door to making new choices that can create a new future for ourselves and our students. That's because when we replay the video of our leadership—when we get present to who we've been being—we begin to notice things that we previously hadn't.

Inside the limitations that pretending imposes on our mindset, all there is to do is wait for the person who's at fault to start being as perfect as we are. And so we wait for the world to change rather than being the change in the world. Inside the pretending, there's nothing else to do.

But as we get present to the behavior, benefit, cost, and pretending, we begin to see the world in new ways. The constraints of the pretending fall away, and ideas that otherwise never would have occurred to us begin to emerge. Now we are able to notice new openings for action that were previously hidden from our view.

Chapter 6
Choice

Why I Do

A principal who attended one of our sessions was so moved that she decided she wanted her entire building to experience the two-day orientation workshop together. This was a surprising request for me—leading an entire school through the workshop at once. I always advise those interested that it is best for 100 percent of the staff to be included in the workshop, but seldom is it requested before I have the chance to advise it. Of course, I was open to the challenge. When I arrived at the school, I was led into the gymnasium, where the entire staff was assembled.

When she said all staff, she clearly meant it. The space was packed with teachers, food service staff, librarians, custodians, paraprofessionals, and even bus drivers. The last group I will never forget because it was immediately obvious that they did not want to be there.

As is often my way when I see people in a workshop clearly experiencing something, I invited the lady who appeared to be the peer leader among the bus drivers to share. Without hesitating, she said, "I don't know why we're wasting our time here. We know how to do our jobs, and this isn't about us."

I thanked her for her comment and for their willingness to be present and then continued to call on others.

Fast forward to the end of the second day. As we were inviting closing comments, the lead bus driver—unprompted—raised her hand to be heard. An immediate hush fell across the entire gym as people, myself included, were suddenly very curious about what we were about to hear.

"I thought my job was to drive kids in a bus, but that's not it. It's what I do, but it's not my job or why I do it. My job is to get students ready to learn, and what happens while they're on my bus makes them either ready to learn or harder to teach."

There was a reverent moment of complete silence as she made her statement. Then, just as completely, everyone in the gymnasium started clapping. What happened in that moment in that gymnasium was more powerful than many recognize.

Mindset We Choose

The bus driver's statement perfectly demonstrates the power of choice in restorative practices. Every member of a school community, from teachers to bus drivers to students, has a role in shaping the environment that prepares students for learning. The mindset we choose is simply a way of viewing the world. But this story also shows the subtle power of mindset in that it colors how we make meaning of what is occurring around us. As the meaning-making changes, our behaviors shift in response to the meaning we've made.

When a student does poorly on a math quiz, we can make that mean that they don't care about math and are being lazy, or we can make it mean that the student doesn't understand and needs support. When we drive the school bus, we can make it mean that we have to get kids from point A to point B, or we can make it mean that our job is to prepare children to learn. The circumstances in the moment have not changed. And as before, none of these ways of viewing the world is good, bad, right, or wrong. There is not enough information to make any such judgment. What is certain, however, is that each different mindset gives rise to very different behaviors. When we see the student as lazy, we're likely to behave differently than when we see them as needing support. When we see our job as preparing children to learn, we're likely to behave differently than when we see our job as moving widgets from point A to point B.

How we show up—who we are being in the moment—is deterministic of the results we create. Who we are being is born of the mindset we choose and how much time and focus we give it.

Currency and Choice

Just like the lead bus driver, in each moment we get to choose who we are being and how we are showing up based on the mindset we're living into. The more minutes we invest in a given mindset, the more our behaviors align with it. Mindset multiplied by minutes. This is about how we invest our time.

Choices

Everything you have is because you (or someone else) traded time to get it. If you have an apple, it's because you traded a small amount of your time to go to the orchard and pick one. Or you went to the store and gave them money, and they gave you an apple. But that money is simply stored time; your job gave you that money in exchange for your time. Even complicated financial products all come down to borrowing someone else's stored time or betting on someone else's profitable use of their time. We invented money to simplify the trading of goods and services across asynchronous value exchanges (if I have some apples to trade and you have a computer to trade, we have a problem that money as currency is well suited to help solve). In the end, money is just stored time; time is just a currency for us to invest. The mindset we choose while investing that time plays a major role in the results we create.

Sometimes the exchange of time is less obvious, but it's there nevertheless if you look for it. For example, all things being equal, if your child is going to be operated on for a life-threatening condition, would you rather it be by a specialist surgeon who does the procedure once per week or a generalist physician who does the procedure once per year? Why would you choose the specialist? What assemblage of conditions would have to be true for you to bypass the specialist and pick the generalist instead? What's really at work here is that a specialist has poured more time into a specific knowledge base or skill. As a result, in circumstances where the results are incredibly important, I want to work with a specialist, and typically I'm willing to pay more for a specialist's time to assist with my needs than for a non-specialist's time. It's not that they, as a person, or their time is any more valuable than someone else's—we all have the same twenty-four hours per day. It's that the time they've invested previously makes what they can do with their time more valuable to me in this circumstance. What a specialist can competently do in one hour a non-specialist might not be able to do well even after many, many hours.

All this is to suggest that the concept of maximization is inextricably intertwined with the concepts of how we spend our time and which mindsets we choose to operate from. The more we choose a mindset focused on maximization, the more specialized we'll become at it over time, which opens the door to results that otherwise wouldn't be available. To take advantage of this mindset shift, however, we have to be present enough to make choices rather than simply following the pattern. Because our brains are optimized for rapid, efficient reactions, not intention-aligned choice-making, if we are to deploy a maximization mindset with the time we have, we need to slow things down.

Self-connection practice, as discussed in Chapter 2, slows the machinery down. We teach it to students because it allows them to analyze whether their current mindset that they're investing time in is creating the results they intend. Once the comparison is done, our coaching is to commit to whichever path the student believes is best aligned with their intentions.

For the lead bus driver, there was a pattern of behavior guided by the mindset she'd chosen: just transport children. Part of why she was frustrated by having to attend the workshop initially was because she had invested a significant amount of time—likely much of her career—into that mindset. Getting nudged into examining that mindset wasn't comfortable for her. But she leaned into the conversation rather than away from it. Over the course of those two days, she chose to begin investing her time into a new mindset. The results she was able to create for students were transformed by that simple choice. Time is currency, and choice is simply what we do with the currency we've been given.

Pretending

One other key aspect of choice is that we have it, whether we want it and whether we acknowledge it. When we are not present with our breathing, we still have the choice to breathe—we're simply not using the option that's available to us. But we're still fully accountable for using it or not using it; we remain fully accountable for our own breathing. Similarly, each moment in life is a choice. Whether we are present and actively drive our choices or whether we allow our patterns to run the show, it's still our choice.

There are moments, however, when the story we tell is "I didn't have a choice." Where rather than owning our choices and the results they created, we look for ways to escape culpability. That is what pretending is all about. And the hallmark of pretending is hiding the fact that pretending is happening, from ourselves, to the point that the mindset we choose to operate within feels like an externally imposed condition of which we're merely a victim.

As is often the case in this work, we aren't using the label of "pretending" as a proxy for good or bad or right or wrong. Pretending is just pretending. It is useful to identify moments of pretending, however, because in doing so, we create a space for our tools to work—in particular, the tools of responsibility and accountability. Inside the self-imposed constraints that pretending creates, the tools that we work so hard to inspire in our students wither.

Mindset is a choice. But in the moments that we don't acknowledge having created the existing patterned mindset, we are indulging in pretending, and our power to create the future wanes. When the lead bus driver stated that her job was to drive a bus, she was pretending—she was not fully owning her choice to create that as the context for her work.

Once she acknowledged that she had created the context in which she was currently living, in that moment she was free from the constraints of the old mindset. She got present to the pattern and, in the space of acknowledgement, she got free of the pretending. That allowed her to create something new. "I get students ready to learn" is a choice, and that new choice gave rise to a new future for herself and her students.

Step Two: Commit Leadership

Chapter 7
School System Leadership

Clearing a Path

"This is just something we need to do," the superintendent said to me. While it certainly helped that her school board was in full support of deploying student-led restorative practices throughout the district, it was clear that her interest in student maximization would have existed with or without their support.

"Can we deploy this next year at all our high schools?" she asked quite seriously.

I laughed out loud before exclaiming, "Absolutely not. I'm very grateful for your enthusiasm though."

After a few moments of discussion, she begrudgingly agreed that this work is about hearts and minds—not something given to mandates and rapid deployment. That said, I completely understood her sense of urgency; students were already suffering the effects of a school system culture that was not always well calibrated to their needs. She was wise to want this work implemented immediately. Unfortunately, effective implementation requires patience.

In the weeks that followed, her leadership was instrumental in removing major roadblocks. When we said we'd need a district-wide coordinator to champion the work, she made it happen. When we said we'd need to have schools apply but that they'd need to know she supported the pilot, she communicated her sense of urgency to her principals. When we told her that we'd need to train a significant number of adults before we ever started training a single student, she provided funding to cover subs so that interested teachers could attend.

All the successes that we had getting applicants and beginning the multiyear training and pilot process had their genesis in her system-wide leadership clearing a path. Without it, nothing would have likely survived the institutional malaise or overcome the sometimes significant challenges involved with implementation.

System-Wide Champion

Every school system needs someone in a position of leadership to take a stand and declare that the school system is committed to its students' maximization and to using student-led restorative practices as the strategy to foster it. Such maximization is not something that will happen on its own absent a hardheaded advocate willing to push for this work regardless of the impediments that stand in the way. We refer to this person as the system-wide champion.

A system-wide champion plays a pivotal role in scaling restorative practices across an entire school system. This individual, often a district-level administrator or a highly experienced educator, is tasked with advocating for restorative practices, identifying potential pilot schools, and securing the necessary resources for implementation. Their leadership ensures that restorative practices are not isolated efforts within individual schools but are parts of a cohesive, system-wide strategy. By providing a consistent vision and framework, the champion helps to align policies, procedures, and professional development efforts across the school system.

The effectiveness of a system-wide champion lies in their ability to influence and collaborate with various impacted groups, including school leaders, teachers, family members, community members, and key central office staff. They must possess strong communication and organizational skills to effectively disseminate information and build enthusiasm for restorative practices. Additionally, the champion is responsible for monitoring and evaluating the implementation process, using data to make informed decisions and adjustments. Their role is crucial in fostering a culture of continuous improvement, ensuring that student maximization is integrated into the fabric of the school system's educational philosophy.

Restorative Leadership Team

One of the early tasks of the system-wide champion is to rally a crew of individuals who share their passion for ensuring that student-led restorative practices take hold throughout the school system. This group—the restorative leadership team—is the backbone of a school's restorative practices efforts. Comprising administrators, teachers, students, and sometimes family or community members, the restorative leadership team is responsible for planning, implementing, and monitoring restorative practices across the school system. The restorative leadership team collaborates to create a shared vision, develop policies, and ensure professional development opportunities that support the school system's restorative intentions.

Effective restorative leadership teams operate with a clear structure and defined roles, ensuring that responsibilities are distributed and that the team functions cohesively. Regular meetings—often weekly at the beginning of a pilot initiative and eventually quarterly as implementation gets rolling—and open communication channels are essential for the restorative leadership team to stay aligned and promptly address challenges. The restorative leadership team also plays a critical role in fostering a restorative mindset among staff and students, leading by example, and providing ongoing support. Through their leadership, the restorative leadership team cultivates a school system culture that allows restorative practices to thrive.

Casting a Student-Led Vision

For the restorative leadership team to be effective at casting a vision for student leadership, they must learn to trust students to take an active role in shaping their school environment and culture. This vision recognizes students as key impacted groups who deserve a voice, as experts regarding their educational experience who deserve to be consulted, and as leaders in the restorative practices implementation process. By involving students in the planning and implementation of restorative work, school systems capture the unique insights students bring to the table and foster a sense of agency and accountability. This approach not only enhances the effectiveness of restorative practices but also promotes the use of the very tools necessary for the work.

Too often, adults attempt to use a vision for student leadership as another means of control by determining which students are involved. An authentic vision for student leadership accepts that the students who are playing leadership roles need to be selected by students, not adults. The inaugural group of student leaders involved in deploying this work throughout the school system will almost invariably be selected by adults. But beyond that, systems will need to be put into place that allow for students to select their own representatives.

Casting a Restorative Vision

Casting a vision for restorative practices requires a commitment to abandoning retribution as the primary response to student behavior. That might sound lovely, but in reality, it is extremely challenging, particularly for the reasons described in Chapter 3. To overcome these challenges, the restorative leadership team will need to articulate a clear and compelling narrative about the importance of maximization and the benefits of restorative practices, as well as describe how both are aligned with the school system's broader goals for improving student outcomes.

To do so, the more inclusive the restorative leadership team is in crafting and communicating the school system's restorative vision—and the transition away from the retributive norm—the more effective it will be. Attaining the needed level of inclusion—bringing together school leaders, staff, students, families, and the broader community—involves providing education and training to ensure that everyone is equipped to participate in the conversation in an informed manner.

Restorative Policy Framework

Another challenge with schools being able to implement student-led restorative practices is that the student code of conduct for most school systems pulls directly from the retributive playbook. Therefore, one of the system-wide restorative leadership team's key tasks is to create a framework that outlines the principles, procedures, and protocols to guide the implementation of restorative practices that will be common across schools throughout the school system. Such a framework is essential for embedding restorative practices within the structural and operational fabric of a school system.

Then, because much of student-led restorative practices implementation will vary by school, each restorative leadership team will need to tailor the implementation to best fit their particular school.

Developing such a framework of restorative policies involves collaboration among school leaders, teachers, students, and community impacted groups to ensure that policies are comprehensive and inclusive. It should also provide clear guidelines for when and how restorative practices are used, delineate the roles and responsibilities of staff and students, and outline processes for training and professional development. Additionally, it should include mechanisms for monitoring and evaluating the effectiveness of restorative practices, allowing for continuous improvement. And yes, it should indicate when it's appropriate to use retributive methods as a primary intervention vs. when they should be used as a secondary or tertiary intervention. By establishing a robust policy framework, the restorative leadership team can create a sustainable and scalable approach to student-led restorative practices that enhances both the school climate and student outcomes.

Funding Professional Development

Once the vision is cast, the culture created, and a framework idealized, the champion and restorative leadership team may discover they are faced with a few additional and substantial challenges. One of them is money. Without resources to provide for the pilot, there's almost no way that this work can take hold. And individual schools won't have the budget to make it through the startup phase. Either the system-wide champion and restorative leadership team secure the funding, or the work is unlikely to happen. And the unexpectedly expensive aspect of starting this work? Professional development.

The reason professional development is often missed as a major cost driver is because the intention is for 100 percent of students and 100 percent of staff to be trained. All of them. That includes every single adult involved with the school and, as seen in Chapter 6, that includes some of the adults outside of the building. Custodial staff, food service staff, transportation staff, as well as teachers, counselors, and everyone else. When we recommend training everyone, we mean *everyone*!

For teachers, that typically means using up all the annual training time, providing a stipend for them to attend training outside of class time and annual training time, or providing a substitute teacher so that they can go to training during class time. Whichever of the three options you pick, the price tag is steep.

Training all students is often no less expensive. My preferred approach to high school trainings is a three-day lock-in for forty to sixty students at a time in a retreat facility designed for training purposes. That entails paying staff, providing a lot of food to a lot of teenagers, and covering the costs associated with the facility. Then multiply that by however many groups of students there are.

The reality is that the costs associated with professional development to start the initiative are fairly steep, and individual schools can't be expected to cover them with their normal budget. When everyone is trained once, the costs of training the people who are new to the building each year tend to be much more manageable. But the first two to three years require a significant investment.

Prioritizing Student-Led Restorative Practices

Another threat to implementation that is uniquely the responsibility of the system-wide champion and restorative leadership team is the routine changes in priorities that often afflict school systems. Too often, the shiny thing of the month comes along, and suddenly strategies that were important yesterday are gone today. Sadly, I've watched this phenomenon happen over and over again. It frequently comes down to this: either the system-wide champion has the authority to hold the line on this work or they don't. Consider this when thinking about who the ideal champion might be. Unfortunately, for every step lower into the administrative ranks of the school system the champion is, the more vulnerable this work becomes.

One scenario I've seen that was helpful was when, at the encouragement of the superintendent, metrics related to this work were adopted by the school board as priorities on which the school board evaluated the superintendent. I give examples of ideas like this in my book *Great On Their Behalf: Why School Boards Fail, How Yours Can Become Effective*.

Whether the priorities are institutionalized by the school board, the superintendent, or an advocate elsewhere within the school system, what matters most is that the mechanisms are put in place for this to be a five-to-ten-year effort, not a five-to-ten-week effort.

Honoring Agreements

At the beginning of this chapter, I introduced the concept of a champion and the cascading effect of having a restorative leadership team. However, the enthusiasm, interest, and dedication it takes to make restorative practices happen in a school is not a linear path. There will be setbacks, and adjustments will be made. How do we ensure the project continues even when enthusiasm, interest, and dedication wane?

The restorative leadership team has to believe that their word matters, and that they have given their word that restorative practices will happen. Inspiring system-wide shifts requires people to agree to do the work and then to honor their word. When school leaders fall into procrastination, push deadlines, or waiver in their support, they decrease the power of their word. When leaders choose to behave this way, it makes it harder to access the intention of the work. None of this is good/bad or right/wrong, but it does have an impact on the work. Common strategies leaders can engage in to avert stops and starts include:

- Communicating any delays, changes, or doubts about the work to the team.
- Understanding that when you are tempted to put something off because you have a reason to, you actually have a choice to honor your agreement or not.
- Create the "why" of your support for this work. Refer to it any time you don't communicate with others or experience a desire to put off, delay, or change the program because of your reasons. This will give you the power to honor your agreements.

Embracing these types of behaviors will increase the pace of your work. This type of leadership and support within a school is not built in a day or a week. It's why this is a multi-year effort and why students need you to start today.

Chapter 8
School-Based Leadership

The Last Step

I had been incredibly interested in visiting a particular school for some time. Finally there, while walking through the hallway, my excitement grew. Just being in the building, it was evident that something different was going on.

I'd been told, "Pretty much all behavior situations that teachers don't choose to manage on their own go directly to our students first. We want our assistant principals supporting instruction, not policing behavior." It was a powerful statement about what the school was committed to creating.

This school had been implementing a student-led approach to restorative practices for several years with an amazing assistant principal as their champion. Through her leadership, students had been systematically trained in and then entrusted with guiding circles throughout the building. Community circles were used to create a sense of belonging in an effort to prevent drama from going unaddressed and becoming something more. Mediation circles were used to address conflicts when they cropped up. Restorative circles were used to address situations when students had dishonored their agreements and caused harm. And all this work was quietly strengthening the students' maximization tools.

Toward the end of my visit, I got to sit down with a group of students who served as the leadership body for this work. "What makes you all confident that this work will continue or that the adults are serious about supporting your leadership?" I asked as the conversation got deeper.

In response, one of the students laughed. "You don't know, do you?" he asked. Then he revealed something that was as powerful as it is rare: "We're the last step in the hiring process. Adults don't get to work here unless this group is confident that they are committed to student leadership."

That's when it became clear why the students in this building had so completely embraced full responsibility for creating a culture and climate of high expectations in their school. One of the most transformative things the adult leaders in a school can do—that this leader had done in this school—is to authentically partner with their students regarding leadership of the school.

School-Based Champion

The need for a champion, someone who embraces, as a matter of personal identity, the ownership of ensuring that this work actually happens, is reaffirmed every time I see a school be successful with their student-led implementation. Each champion plays a pivotal role in the successful implementation of student-led restorative practices. Simply put, without them it's not going to happen.

This individual, often a dedicated assistant principal, counselor, or highly influential teacher, serves as the key advocate and leader for restorative initiatives or student leadership within the school. They typically take responsibility for coordinating training sessions, facilitating the school's first circles, and constantly nudging for the school's policies to align with restorative practices. By modeling restorative practices in their interactions and decision-making processes, the school-based champion sets a standard for the entire school community. Their leadership is crucial in maintaining momentum and enthusiasm for the restorative approach and for a student-leadership approach, as well as for ensuring that it becomes an integral part of the school culture rather than the flavor of the month.

The effectiveness of a school-based champion lies in their ability to bridge the gap between theory and practice. They must possess a deep understanding of restorative principles and be skilled in the tools that this work seeks to promote: accountability, responsibility, self-regulation, metacognition, empathy, and active listening. Their role also involves ongoing support and mentorship for both students and reluctant staff, helping them navigate challenges and celebrate successes. The most effective champions are stubborn enough not to be deterred by pessimism while reflective enough to be open to pivoting when the circumstances require it.

Restorative Leadership Team

A champion's first initiative in this work is to bring together a coalition of interested people with willing hearts and minds; you can't force people into restoration. But it's highly unlikely that an entire building of adults will already be onboard from day one with the idea of transitioning from an adult-led approach to a student-led approach, from a retributive approach to a restorative approach. More often than not, the wisest course of action is to start by identifying the adults who *are* already fired up about the possibility of making the transition and then build out a collective desire for the transition.

Developing such a coalition of the willing is essential for starting a student-led restorative practices initiative. It will take a stalwart group of individuals eager to invest their time and energy into its implementation. By bringing together a diverse group of impacted groups who already bought into the concept, the champion increases the likelihood that restorative practices are supported from multiple angles and integrated into various aspects of school life. Don't squander precious time trying to convince the hardened skeptics and retribution devotees; their time in the process will come.

The strength of your initial coalition lies in its ability to harness the unique perspectives and skills of its members, so be certain to break out of your limited circle of acquaintances. One way to do this is to create an opportunity for people to come and learn about what student-led restorative practices are. This is where inviting a certified student-led restorative practices coach to come lead an introductory session could help. Another way is to take members of your school community to observe another school that is already doing the work.

After a champion has pushed for a coalition of the willing and the coalition has begun the task of introducing this work to the full staff, it's time to formally create the school's restorative leadership team. The restorative leadership team is the body that takes formal accountability for ensuring the student-led restorative practices are effectively deployed throughout the school. Among their duties are conducting quarterly self-evaluations to see where implementation is at, shepherding implementation, ensuring that as close as possible to 100 percent of students have access to training, and ensuring that as close as possible to 100 percent of staff have access to training.

Inspiring Staff Excitement

Training the staff isn't enough. If the school's staff isn't excited about this work, the work won't last. Sure, it may get started, but it will get ended quickly. I've simply never seen a student-led restorative practices initiative fail because of the students. If it fails, it fails because the adults were not excited about doing the work. It's the job of the champions to build the initial coalition; it's the job of the coalition to build excitement among the rest of the staff.

To join the movement, school staff must believe in the value of restorative practices and be willing to shift from traditional retributive approaches. While this transition often requires comprehensive training, nothing seems to speed it nearly as quickly as seeing the work in action. Once you see what students who are doing this work are capable of, you can never fully unsee it. Even if it means borrowing students from another school who have already been doing the work, it's helpful to find a way for the full staff to see the work in action.

The other most effective strategy for building excitement is for staff to have their own experience with the work. Whether that means participating in one of the two-day experiential orientations that certified coaches put on or participating in a student-led circle, anything that puts school based staff in the position to experience the work—not just witness it—will go a long way toward inspiring excitement.

It should go without saying that people tend to prefer the plans that they have a hand in creating. So as the champion and the early coalition begin to rally excitement, it's important to find ways to include others in the planning. This is why the restorative leadership team needs to include a diversity of staff—including staff members who fully believe in the work and staff members who are somewhat skeptical. Creating a supportive environment where staff feel heard and valued is essential in gaining their buy-in. Encouraging open dialogues about the challenges and benefits of restorative practices allows educators to express their thoughts and collaborate on solutions.

Additionally, providing ongoing support and resources, such as access to coaches who have been trained in a student-led approach to restorative practices or dedicated time for planning and reflection, can help ease the transition. Recognizing and celebrating small successes along the way can reinforce the positive impact of restorative practices, gradually building a culture of acceptance and then excitement among staff members.

Communicating with Families

Families cannot be left behind or left out of this conversation. These are their children, so they have a right to know what's going on in the school. There's also the likelihood that families are deeply invested in retributive approaches. Their responses will often range from confused to angry when told that a restorative approach is being considered as the primary approach to culture and climate creation. And that's before you mention that it'll be students leading it.

That is why effective communication with families is a cornerstone of implementing restorative practices in schools. Families need to understand the principles and benefits of restorative practices to fully support and engage with the process. Don't assume families will understand the concept or agree with it. It'll be up to the restorative leadership team to inform and educate families through multiple channels, including newsletters, informational meetings, and workshops. These communications should highlight the tools that this work is focused on and the student outcomes supported by the mastery of these tools. By involving families from the outset, schools can build a partnership with them that reinforces the restorative approach both at school and, often, at home.

Involving families in restorative practices also means providing opportunities for them to participate in the process. Schools can invite families to join community circles as part of family-teacher-student conferences or mediation sessions when appropriate. This inclusion fosters a sense of shared commitment, which can strengthen trust between the school and families. Additionally, workshops for families on student-led restorative practices can equip them with the tools and insights needed to support their children. By maintaining open, honest communication—including making it easy for families to opt out of having their children involved with this process entirely—schools can create a cohesive community committed to student maximization.

Practice, Practice, Practice

If I want to get better at throwing a ball, what do I have to do? Practice! And if I want to get better at playing the piano, what do I have to do? Practice! And if I want students to gain fluency with the tools they'll need to live a choice-filled life, what will they have to do? Yes, practice, practice, practice. The adage "practice makes perfect" is particularly relevant when it comes to implementing restorative practices in schools.

The restorative leadership team will need to prioritize creating routine opportunities for students to practice using their tools. While this can take the form of before and after school club time, lunch time, or other special periods throughout the week, that's not what I recommend.

The ideal scenario creates recurring, daily opportunities for students to be available to do the work and for students to get practice doing the work. For example, in a high school, the ideal practice opportunity would be for the master schedule to include a study hall-type classroom time during each period of the school day. While it might look like an ordinary study hall, in reality it would be populated with students who have already been trained to lead circles. Each period in which there are actual circles that have been referred, the students lead the circles. Each period in which there are not referrals, students do a quick practice circle before using the rest of the period as a study hall. This arrangement ensures that students have plenty of opportunity to practice with their tools *and* that the school has access to circles on an as-needed basis every hour of the school day.

This type of regular and consistent practice is crucial for students to develop the desired fluency with the tools of metacognition, self-regulation, empathy, active listening, accountability, and responsibility. The more students are afforded these types of practice opportunities, the stronger they become. In addition, this level of repetition helps to embed restorative practices into the daily routines of the school, making them a natural and expected part of school life rather than an occasional intervention.

Location, Location, Location

The physical environment where circles take place can significantly influence their effectiveness. When a defined location for this work isn't set, the likelihood of regular practice decreases, and there will be times when a circle is needed but isn't held because an appropriate location can't be found. The restorative leadership team will need to be vigilant about advocating for a permanent, defined space for circles to be practiced and to occur (other than any that are taking place in actual classrooms).

Choosing the right location for restorative circles and mediation sessions is crucial to creating a safe, welcoming, and conducive atmosphere for open dialogue. Students shouldn't need to worry about who is walking past and might see them participating in a circle, who might hear the conversation taking place in the circle, or anything else like that. Ideally, these spaces should be quiet, comfortable, and free from distractions, allowing participants to focus fully on the circle.

Schools should consider creating dedicated spaces for restorative practices, such as a "restorative room" or a designated area within the school that is used exclusively for these purposes. Having a consistent and well-prepared location for circles helps to signal their importance and seriousness to students and staff. It also provides a tangible reminder of the school's commitment to fostering student maximization.

… Step Three: Clarify and Monitor Priorities

Chapter 9
Setting Goals

Focusing on Student Outcomes

Choosing effective goals is always deceptively difficult. As I was working with a team of educators who had volunteered to design this work for their school system, we found ourselves spiraling. After looking at our list of potential goals, I called for us to pull back and reconsider the task we were working on.

"Here are the goal ideas so far," I said, writing them on the board.

- How many students get trained to lead circles each semester
- How many students participate in circles each week
- How many circles are hosted each quarter
- Reductions in referrals written each quarter
- Reductions in in-school suspension each year
- Reductions in out-of-school suspension each year

"We need to focus on the outcomes we want for our students," I reminded them. "At the end of the cycle, what do we want them to know or be able to do as a result of having led circles in school?"

We had been discussing potential goals that were about inputs or outputs, and then we got hung up on adult outcomes rather than student outcomes, so I added that information next to each item:

- How many students get trained to lead circles each semester—student output
- How many students participate in circles each week—student output
- How many circles are hosted each quarter—adult input

- Reductions in referrals written each quarter—adult output
- Reductions in in-school suspension each year—adult outcome
- Reductions in out-of-school suspension each year—adult outcome

With this perspective added to the conversation, the direction began to shift.

"So basically, we need to begin with the end in mind," one of the teachers in the group said, "instead of how we get to the end." She got it exactly: we need goals about student outcomes.

This story reveals an incredibly common misconception about student-led restorative practices. Many want or expect this work to be about changing problematic student behavior or reducing discipline rates, but it's not. It's about maximization—about students gaining the tools necessary to experience the maximal expression of their potential and to live a choice-filled life. Are near-term changes in student behavior and adult behavior common in this work? Absolutely. That reality is a lot of what has kept me excited about and invested in this work.

But this is a specific journey, and if the focus—the goal—becomes the steps along the journey and not the destination we intend, it undermines the likelihood of getting to the destination. The inputs and outputs—or even adult outcomes—can't be allowed to serve as a proxy for inspiring improvements in student outcomes—improvements in what students know or are able to do with tools of maximization.

Why Goals Matter

If we have a destination in mind but we don't communicate it with clarity, others can't help us get there. Imagine telling your taxi driver that it is incredibly important for you to get to your destination quickly, but you don't tell them where the destination is. In this strange scenario, all their knowledge and skills about driving and all their insights into local traffic patterns and secret shortcuts are rendered useless; until you declare the destination, they can't support your intention.

When it comes to restorative practices, often schools want to hop in the car and start moving fast without first getting clear about where they're trying to go. Without first getting clear about the goal, it's common for schools to—no surprise—not reach the destination they wanted. It's important to avoid that trap because when it happens, those who are uncomfortable with student-led work or restorative work will point to it and say, "See? I told you it wouldn't work." This then invites misplaced arguments for why students can't be trusted (permitting a reversion to an adultist mindset) and why restorative practices can't work (permitting a reversion to a retributive mindset).

Further, imagine that we continue to refuse to tell our taxi driver where to take us. So the taxi driver takes us someplace they think would be good for us to go—even though it's not where we want to be. Now we are frustrated because we aren't where we want to be. In that moment, who is responsible for our frustration? Of course it's our own fault, not the fault of the taxi driver! We were always going to be accountable for how things turned out; we chose the taxi driver, after all. But in the moment we chose not to communicate our destination, we further made ourselves responsible for ending up in a place we didn't want to be.

Goals matter because they clarify accountability and responsibility. They inform the next step the restorative leadership team will take in the direction of their school community's vision for what students should know and be able to do. When clear goals are established, we have done our part to be accountable for the results of our vision even as we delegate responsibility to others for implementing individual parts of that vision. When lines of accountability and responsibility are clarified, it's easier to ensure that the restorative initiatives are not just theoretical but are actively practiced and refined over time. Setting and pursuing well-defined goals allows the restorative leadership team to transform the abstract principles of student-led restorative practices into concrete action steps.

Inputs, Outputs, and Outcomes

Understanding the distinction between inputs, outputs, and outcomes is essential when setting goals. Inputs refer to the resources, time, and effort invested into a program or strategy, such as the number of staff trainings provided, the implementation plans, or the materials purchased. Outputs, on the other hand, are the immediate results of these inputs, like the number of circles conducted, the frequency of meetings, or the number of students participating in the circles. While these metrics are very important, as I'll highlight later, they do not directly measure the impact at the end of the cycle. Outcomes are the results measurable at the end of the cycle, after all the inputs and outputs.

> **Inputs** describe measures of the resource or strategy that are observable at the beginning of a cycle.
>
> **Outputs** describe measures of the implementation that are observable in the midst of a cycle.
>
> **Outcomes** describe measures of the results that are observable at the end of a cycle.

When setting goals, the restorative leadership team should focus on getting clear about what outcomes it wants to create at the end of the cycle. By focusing on outcomes, restorative leadership teams can ensure that their efforts are leading to the end results intended. This shift from focusing on inputs and outputs to having goals focused on outcomes requires a deeper level of commitment and reflection but is essential for achieving the true potential of restorative practices. It ensures that the practices are not just implemented but effective in promoting student maximization.

But a focus on outcomes, while necessary, is insufficient. An additional distinction is needed. When setting goals for restorative practices, it's critical to distinguish between student outcomes and adult outcomes. Student outcomes are about what students know or are able to do at the end of the cycle. These outcomes might include summative demonstrations of self-regulation, metacognition, active listening, empathy, responsibility, and accountability. These are the ultimate indicators of success for student-led restorative practices, as they reflect the growth and development of students in ways that prepare them for an agentic and choice-filled future.

Adult outcomes, on the other hand, pertain to the knowledge and skills of the school system's adults: what staff, educators, and administrators know or are able to do. These might include reductions in disciplinary referrals, decreases in suspensions, and changes in how staff navigate conflicts and engage with students. While these outcomes are quite important and can contribute to the success of implementing restorative practices, they are not the reason that student-led restorative practices exist.

None of this is to suggest that adult outcomes are unimportant; they're incredibly important enablers for what we want for students. But they are the means, not the ends. By prioritizing student outcomes, restorative leadership teams can ensure that student-led restorative practices lead to lasting improvements in what students know or are able to do rather than just temporary shifts in adult behavior.

> **Student outcomes** describe measures of the results created by a school system that describe what students know or are able to do and are observable at the end of a cycle.
>
> **Adult outcomes** describe measures of the results created by a school system that are not student outcomes and are observable at the end of a cycle.

SMART Goals

The restorative leadership team's goals can't be flowery platitudes designed to make adults feel good. They need to be specific agreements that the restorative leadership team is making regarding exactly what it will accomplish. And they need to allow the restorative leadership team to know definitively whether progress is being made in the direction of student maximization. To accomplish these things, the restorative leadership team's goals need to be SMART.

SMART goals—specific, measurable, attainable, results-focused, and time-bound—are essential for effectively guiding restorative practices in schools. Goals that are specific allow the restorative leadership team to clearly define what is to be achieved, providing direction and focus. Measurable goals include criteria to track implementation progress and assess students' growth with the tools in ways that are quantifiable. Attainable goals are realistic and achievable, taking into consideration the resources and constraints of the school system. Results-focused goals are exclusively about student outcomes—never adult outcomes—ensuring that each goal contributes meaningfully to measuring student maximization. Goals that are time-bound set deadlines for when the goals will be achieved, creating a sense of urgency and prompting consistent effort.

For a goal to meet all of the criteria for being SMART, it must at a minimum have six elements:

- Starting date: The first month and day the goal is measured
- Ending date: The last month and day the goal is measured
- Starting point: How many students demonstrate the student outcome on the starting date

- Ending point: How many students demonstrate the student outcome on the ending date
- Population: The group of students being measured
- Measure: The instrument used to provide the student outcome's starting and ending points

When all of these elements are in place and the resulting goal is attainable, we typically say that the goal is SMART. Examples of potential SMART goals that focus on student outcomes—measures of what students know or are able to do at the end of the cycle—include:

- The number of student facilitators who effectively facilitated, as defined by the student-led restorative practices guide, thirty or more circles will increase from X in June 2025 to Y by June 2028.
- The percentage of freshmen who effectively demonstrated active listening and empathy, as defined by the student-led restorative practices guide, will increase from X percent in June 2025 to Y percent by June 2030.
- The percentage of students who have been suspended more than ten days during their secondary career who effectively facilitated at least ten mediation or restorative circles will increase from X percent in June 2025 to Y percent by June 2028.
- The number of high school students who effectively demonstrated self-regulation and metacognition will increase from X percent in June 2025 to Y percent by June 2029.
- The number of graduates who effectively taught responsibility and accountability to their classmates will increase from X percent in June 2025 to Y percent by June 2030.

These are only meant as examples, not exemplars. Each restorative leadership team will have to listen to its school community and evaluate its students' needs and, from that, develop a set of one to three goals that are responsive to their circumstances and that last the length of their implementation plan, which is typically three to five years.

Developing Goals

When the restorative leadership team is setting SMART goals about student outcomes, it will need two primary pieces of information: a summary of relevant data about students—particularly anything that the restorative leadership team believes speaks to where they are on their path toward maximization—and a summary of input from the school community.

To create a summary of school community input, an effective goal development process for student-led restorative practices requires hearing from all impacted groups, including students, educators, and often families and community members. A collaborative approach ensures that the goals reflect the vision of the entire school community and increases the likelihood of the community embracing and owning the work. The process typically begins with providing as many people as possible with training about student-led restorative practices via a two- or three-day initial orientation session. The more people who understand the work, the easier it will be for them to get excited about the work and to support the implementation of the work.

There are many different approaches to creating a summary of student data. I offer one example here, but it should be considered simply that: one example, not *the* way to do it. That said, an approach to student data analysis that I've enjoyed involves first brainstorming the strengths of their student body when regarding their ability to fully experience their maximum potential and the gaps, or unrealized opportunities. Once strengths and opportunities are identified, then we do a root cause analysis by asking, for each individual strength and each individual opportunity, five whys. For example, if an opportunity is "accountability," then the restorative leadership team should ask, "Why is accountability one of the key opportunities?" Then, take whatever the answer is and ask, "Why is that?" Then ask again. Ask why five times. Whatever you get at the end has a decent chance of being a root cause. Once you have root causes, start to look for patterns and any school system data that meaningfully correlates with the patterns. Often this process is described as looking for a needle in a haystack. That's not entirely wrong. But these are needles worth finding since they will help point toward which student needs are the greatest and which student needs, if met, would have the greatest leverage in supporting the student body's journey toward maximization.

With both one-to-five-page summaries in hand—community listening and student data—the restorative leadership team is ready to use that data to set its SMART goals about student outcomes.

Developing Interim Goals

It won't be enough to have just end goals. By design, those goals are about student outcomes, which means they won't be knowable until the end of the cycle. Therefore, the restorative leadership team needs a way to monitor progress throughout the school year. For that purpose, it adopts student output measures that are predictive of the goals and that are updateable throughout the year. We refer to these metrics as interim goals.

Interim goals are crucial for maintaining momentum. These progress measures break down larger, more ambitious goals into manageable steps, providing clear milestones that can be achieved in a shorter time frame. Developing interim goals involves identifying specific student outputs that will contribute to the overall success of the restorative leadership team's goals. Like the goals with which they are aligned, interim goals are also SMART: specific, measurable, attainable, results-focused, and time-bound.

For instance, here is an example of a goal:

- The percentage of underclassmen who are more than one grade level behind in ELA who effectively demonstrated active listening and metacognition, as defined by the student-led restorative practices guide, will increase from X percent in June 2025 to Y percent by June 2028.

Examples of interim goals might include the following:

- The percentage of rising freshmen and freshmen who participated in at least a student-led restorative practices weeklong training during the summer or three-day orientation during the school year will increase from X percent in July 2025 to Y percent by July 2027.
- The number of sophomores who are more than one grade level behind in ELA who have effectively led a mediation circle, as defined by the student-led restorative practices guide, will increase from X in October 2025 to Y by October 2027.
- The number of underclassmen who have co-led a student-led restorative practices training for their classmates or for adults will increase from X in October 2025 to Y by October 2027.

Again, these are just examples, not exemplars. The intention is to show what student-led restorative practices-aligned student outputs might look like.

Once the restorative leadership team sets their goals and interim goals, they are able to use some of their time each month reviewing their interim goals to determine whether or not these interim goals are on track. The next chapter describes this process.

Chapter 10
Monitor What Matters

Who's to Blame?

It's not enough to think you have improved. You need to know for certain whether you have or not. This is the purpose of the self-evaluation instrument in the student-led restorative practices implementation guide.

> www.StudentLedRP.org/instrument/

    As a certified student-led restorative practices coach, I often get invited to sit in on restorative leadership team meetings to help problem-solve and answer questions. During one such meeting, the team was struggling to figure out why it felt like implementation had slowed down. Everyone had a theory.

    A student wondered if it was the principal's fault. A teacher wondered if it was the central office's fault. A counselor wondered if it was my fault. All of these were reasonable theories, but they lacked one important thing: evidence. This is when I asked what their last quarterly self-evaluation score was and what their current quarter's self-evaluation score was. After a few moments of asking around, they finally remembered the last quarter's rating, but they realized that they hadn't conducted a self-evaluation for this quarter. They had a shared feeling that something wasn't working, but they hadn't used the tools at their disposal to help identify why.

    So we pulled out their school system's version of the student-led restorative practices guide and started going through the self-evaluation together. Very quickly, it became obvious exactly where they had slowed down.

Then we were able to brainstorm about next steps to address the areas of challenge. I then invited them to identify who specifically was going to own each next step and by when they would have it addressed. By the time we ended the session, I could see the enthusiasm return as the feeling of frustration was supplanted with a feeling of agency. That transition in how the work is experienced is a large part of the benefit of conducting routine monitoring– of both the outputs aligned to the outcomes (progress monitoring) and the inputs aligned to the outputs (self-evaluation).

Why Monitoring Matters

It's often said in the education world that what gets measured gets done. This is not far off the mark. Our version goes like this: the frequency of monitoring gives rise to the frequency of pivoting. If the results we want for our students require us to adjust to their reality, the likelihood of adjustment is directly tied to whether we have systems in place to track how our strategies and our students are doing—and then take action according to what the data tells us.

Having a system for monitoring in place requires two forms of tracking: tracking our efforts (self-evaluation) and tracking our effects (progress monitoring). Tracking our efforts helps us understand whether we are actually implementing the strategies we said we would implement. Tracking our effects helps us understand whether our strategies are creating the result we intend.

Tracking Our Effort: Self-Evaluation

For the restorative leadership team to know whether it is effectively deploying student-led restorative practices, it needs to self-evaluate. That involves looking at the set of inputs the restorative leadership team has chosen to see if their implementation is creating the outputs the restorative leadership team intends. The primary tool that the restorative leadership team uses for self-evaluation is the student-led restorative practices implementation instrument.

The student-led restorative practice's implementation instrument is made up of six competencies of an effective restorative leadership team: focus mindset, commit leadership, clarify and monitor priorities, community circles, mediation circles, and restorative circles. Each month—or, at absolute minimum, each quarter—the restorative leadership team reviews what it has done over the previous month and looks to see where that lands on the instrument. The instrument is designed to reveal a score between zero and one hundred that describes how focused the restorative leadership team is on implementing student-led restorative practices.

Importantly, self-evaluation is not about good, bad, right, or wrong. The response to a low score or stagnation isn't that the people on the restorative leadership team are bad; that view of self-evaluation is counterproductive. Instead, a low score or a stagnant score simply provides signals to the restorative leadership team that what it's doing isn't yet working and to try something new. Said differently, the frequency of monitoring gives rise to the frequency of pivoting.

Self-evaluation is about continuous improvement, not condemnation or blame. The data tells you what the data tells you, and it's up to you to choose to be responsive to the data or not.

> To view the most current version of the student-led restorative practices implementation instrument, visit www.StudentLedRP.org/instrument/

Effective Self-Evaluation

The student-led restorative practices implementation instrument is best used by the full restorative leadership team (and, the first few times, with support from a certified student-led restorative practices coach). After receiving an orientation to the framework, each restorative leadership team member should individually score the entire team on each competency.

After the very first time that each restorative leadership team member has scored the team individually, whoever is facilitating the self-evaluation will lead the leadership team through a collective scoring process to establish a starting point. This baseline provides clarity about the restorative leadership team's current strengths and weaknesses relative to implementing their restorative vision.

Once a starting point has been set, the restorative leadership team should schedule regular self-evaluations every three months to track progress. Ideally, each quarter will show meaningful increases in the restorative leadership team's focus on implementing student-led restorative practices, aiming for a score of eighty or higher within the first two years. Restorative leadership teams attempting this work without the support of a trained coach often struggle; the behavior changes required are significant, and expert guidance is critical for success.

It is normal to experience resistance to tracking effort using a self-evaluation tool. It is much easier to affix blame "out there" than to take responsibility for one's actions. It is much easier to point a finger at someone else. Evaluation and assessment often get wrapped up in good/bad/right/wrong and easily collapse into judgment. People may resist evaluation because they don't want to be judged. Approaching self-evaluation without judgment requires clearing away those preconceptions before the assessment begins. Invite participants to talk about their fears. Perhaps they feel inadequate, that they'll reveal something they don't want known, or that they feel like an imposter to evaluate anything—all common resistance mechanisms. Once the team faces any of those fears that are present, they have space to be responsible. It is less likely that fingers will be pointed or blame assigned when there is a path to judgment-free responsibility.

Tracking Our Effect: Progress Monitoring

For the restorative leadership team to know whether its strategies are effectively creating the results it intends, it needs to progress monitor. This involves looking at the set of outputs the restorative leadership team has chosen to see if they are moving in the direction of the outcomes they've chosen. The primary tool the restorative leadership team uses for progress monitoring is the interim goals (the outputs) and the goals (the outcomes).

Progress monitoring is best conducted after the restorative leadership team has self-evaluated since that is often valuable data for the following steps. Once that is complete, the restorative leadership team chair is accountable for the creation of a one-to-five-page monitoring report—less is often more—that details four things:

- **The Priority**: What specifically is the subject of the monitoring report? Is it one of the interim goals, or is it the goal itself? If monitoring monthly, only monitor one interim goal at a time. If monitoring quarterly, do two or three. Monthly monitoring is recommended.
- **The Data**: What is the current status of the interim goal or goal being monitored? When available, include the data from the previous three reporting periods and the current reporting period, as well as the desired ending point data. These should be placed on a line graph or similar visualization tool that makes it easy for the

restorative leadership team to see whether performance is improving, stagnant, or declining.
- **The Interpretation**: What is the restorative leadership team chair's view of what the data means? Typically, this is just red/yellow/green, one to five stars, or a descriptive indicator—on track/near track/off track—that succinctly describes the chair's view of current performance based on what the data is telling them.
- **The Plan**: What action steps are recommended based on what the data means? It's most useful for the chair to explain their view of the challenges the restorative leadership team faces and their view of the optimal responses to those challenges and then identify one to three high-leverage next steps that they believe will allow for the optimal response.

The restorative leadership team should review the monitoring report and discuss which next steps it will take, who will be accountable for them, and by when they are committing that they will be complete.

Effective Progress Monitoring

Too often in public education, leaders do not pay sufficient attention to what's working and what's not working. The result can be a revolving door of initiatives, programs, or "silver bullets" that drain resources, frustrate staff, and fail students. Breaking this cycle requires having clearly agreed-upon data, a predictable cadence of reviewing the data to see what's working and what's not, and the expectation that this information impacts what happens next. Effective progress monitoring accomplishes all of those things.

Progress monitoring is a conversation led by the restorative leadership team chair among the restorative leadership team members that provides members with the opportunity to evaluate the alignment between their intention (goals) and current performance (reality). While goals and reality may not match perfectly, it only becomes problematic when there is no evidence of growth. And even if growth isn't yet occurring, that's only catastrophic if the restorative leadership team doesn't have sufficiently aggressive strategies in place for making progress.

When having the monitoring conversation, here are a few key things for restorative leadership team members to keep in mind:

- **Lead by Example**: Restorative leadership team behavior can set the culture for a school. If restorative leadership team members want a culture where all school community members are reflective in their behaviors, they set the stage for that by demonstrating what it looks like for the restorative leadership team to be open and reflective as well.
- **Clarify Strategies**: When the restorative leadership team receives monitoring reports from the chair, the report should be at a sixth grade level and include how the restorative leadership team might respond to the data. If the data says things are slightly off track, the chair's recommended next steps should reflect that. If the data says that performance is completely off track, the chair's recommended strategies should reflect the urgency that the current reality demands.

Step Four: Practice Community Circles

Chapter 11
Creating Belonging

Psychological Safety

At the beginning of sessions with my staff, I often form a circle and do an integrity check-in. It always begins with me identifying a moment in the previous twenty-four hours when I didn't honor my word or I didn't honor what I allowed people to expect of me. Once I share about my behavior's lack of integrity, then I share about the benefit to me in the moment, the cost to others, and what I was pretending. After I speak, the person on my left or right takes a turn, and then we proceed around the circle. We are so present and so transparent that even with fifteen to twenty people on staff, the entire check-in-style community circle only takes three or four minutes.

Once we go around the circle, the floor becomes open for anyone to share. Often staff notice patterns in the sharing and offer support, or one person's sharing triggers a reflection for someone else. A consistent side effect of our integrity check-ins is that situations of hiding vital issues from each other or pretending we'd honored our agreements regarding one of our responsibilities when we hadn't are much less likely because we have created a space that is psychologically safe enough to address things as they come up.

Often when new staff experience our community circles for the first time, they worry about how they look or about losing face. But in the community that we co-created, the result of our check-ins is more trust, more openness, and more willingness to believe in each other. The result is the experience of belonging.

Even as years have passed, these circles have played a significant role in generating a sense of belonging that has lingered. Recently a staff member got married, and not surprisingly, a large group of former staff showed up to celebrate along with him. When we all saw each other, we immediately came together to take a staff photo just like the old days.

Create and Behave

As I mentioned in Chapter 1, belonging describes the choice to create and behave from seeing others as having a generous mindset toward you. The experience of belonging is incredibly powerful. Inside the context of belonging, you experience being seen, valued, and wanted. So even when challenges come up in your relationships with others, since you've already created the idea that they view you generously, your behavior is driven by that.

Creating and sustaining a culture of belonging requires deliberate action and consistency. For my staff, it was essential that we continuously modeled these behaviors in our daily interactions. Our community circles built a foundation of community that permeated all aspects of our work together. When staff members saw that it was not only safe but also encouraged to admit mistakes, seek support, and offer support, the environment allowed us to show up more powerfully for the students we served. It became a community where people felt valued and seen, not just for their successes but for their authentic selves, flaws and all.

One of the most profound effects of this culture is the way it empowers staff to take risks and innovate without fear of judgment or retribution. Knowing that they belong and that their contributions are valued makes staff more willing to push boundaries and explore new ideas. When staff feels safe and supported, they are more likely to collaborate and share insights. This collective sense of belonging fuels our success, enabling us to achieve more together than any of us could have on our own. These are direct consequences of us creating and behaving within the context of belonging that our community circles serve to inspire.

About Community Circles

When community is desired, the maximization-aligned approach involves creating belonging among the students involved. The student-led restorative practice used to accomplish belonging is the community circle. Student-led community circles describe 1) a conversation facilitated by students as part of school community routine, 2) where the choice is made to use belonging as the strategy for community, and 3) where the participants have choice and equal voice. For every one hundred student-led circles a school conducts, ideally around eighty of those will be community circles. When 80 percent of the circles taking place throughout the week are community circles that are focused on building a healthy learning community, ideally there becomes a reduced need for mediation circles and restorative circles.

Student-led community circles are distinct from class meetings or other student meetings often used to convey information from a central source to participants where the priority is hierarchical information distribution. Such a scenario would not be appropriate within the context of a community circle. In addition, community circles are distinct in that students are leading the conversation rather than adults, since a large part of the intention is to ensure students develop the tools they need to experience maximization.

Community circles are most appropriate when there is a routine and ongoing need to create community among participants. The following chapter presents one example of how a community circle might go. It is important that student facilitators are fully trained to lead all of the following steps; they should not have to rely on adults for any of the steps in the pre-circle, circle, or post-circle.

Chapter 12
Implementing Community Circles

Pre-Circle
Before a circle can start, the facilitator needs to ensure that the circumstances are healthy for a circle to be held. The following elements should be present each time a circle is needed:

- **Co-Facilitator**: Student facilitators should never enter a circle solo. For a community circle, there is at least one student co-facilitator in the circle who can provide support to the student facilitator.
- **Function**: Student facilitators collaborate with their fellow students and any participating adults to determine what, if any, special function the circle will perform in addition to the overall benefit of creating community. In addition to typical community circles, common additional functions include, but are not limited to, participants experiencing community around:
    - **Academics**: Participants share about where they are relative to a specific course or assignment.
    - **Celebration**: Participants honor accomplishments of other participants.
    - **Check-In**: Participants see how other participants are doing.
    - **Decision-Making**: Participants collectively identify options and then choose among them.
    - **Gratitude**: Participants share appreciation about other participants.

- **Integrity**: Participants acknowledge where they haven't honored their agreements and then recommit.
- **Logistics**: The student co-facilitator ensures that the space is appropriate for a circle and is set up for a circle and that the time, date, and location have been confirmed with all participants. Sometimes teachers will request for community circles to take place during instructional time as a strategy to support the lesson plan; much of the time community circles will take place away from core instructional time.
- **Agreement**: For recurring circles, such as those in specific classrooms, the facilitator can rely on existing agreements that are in place. For non-recurring circles, such as special groups or activities, the facilitator can create some initial norms that can be validated by the full group later.

Circle

Facilitator Self-Connection

Student facilitators need to regulate themselves before they can create a space for community with others. While there are many techniques for accomplishing self-regulation, the tool we train on the most is self-connection practice. This is typically done silently but can be done out loud as well.

- **Awareness**: Observe Breath: The facilitator observes their breathing and gets present with themselves.
- **Acknowledgment**: Identify Feelings: The facilitator identifies the physical or emotional experience they're having in the moment.
  - Examples include "I feel..." or "The sensation in my body is..."
    - "I feel upset. My body feels tense and tight."
    - "I feel scattered and overwhelmed."
    - "I feel anxious, insecure, and not heard."
- **Acknowledgment**: Identify Needs: The facilitator identifies what met or unmet need the feeling is pointing to.
  - Examples include "I need..." or "My need for _____ is/isn't met."
    - "I need to calm myself."

- "My need for clarity is not met around what I'm supposed to do."
- "I need to take a break and have the chance to refocus."
- **Aligned Action**: Declare Commitment: The facilitator identifies a specific action that they can take in the moment that would be a step in the direction of meeting the unmet need or honoring the met need. Ideal commitments are SMART and can be measured or observed during the next seven days.
  - Examples include "I commit to..." or "The commitment I'm making to myself is..."
    - "I can calm myself down when I am feeling upset. I commit to using self-connection the next three times I'm feeling upset."
    - "I commit to asking for directions from my teacher during the next five school days."
    - "I can control my impulses when I am tempted to act on them. I commit to stopping and taking a breath before responding the next five times John or one of his friends talks to me."

Facilitator Creates Circle (dependent on how the circle is being used)

Ideally, the agreements necessary for the circle to be successful are already part of the classroom's or group's norms.
- **Prior Agreements**: "Our normal agreements that are particularly important for the circle are..."
- **Additional Agreements**: "Are there any additional agreements that you need in order to participate?" and then "Which of these do we all agree on?"
- **Check for Agreement**: "Is there anyone who does not agree to these agreements?"

Facilitator Starts Circle (dependent on how the circle is being used)

- **Gratitude**: "When you did [insert observation], I felt [insert word that describes a feeling]."

- **Integrity**: "I said I would [insert prior commitment], but I did not. What you can expect is [insert new commitment]."
- **Academic**: "As we go around the circle, on a scale from one to ten, how comfortable are you with [insert assignment, lesson, etc.]?" or "Which aspect of [insert assignment, lesson, etc.] are you feeling most comfortable or most uncomfortable with?"
- **Check-In**: "As we go around the circle, on a scale from one to ten, how are you feeling today?" or "How are you feeling today?" or "Which aspect of [insert area of life, school, work, etc.] are you feeling most comfortable or most uncomfortable with?"
- **Celebration**: "What do you most want to celebrate today?" or "Which aspect of [insert area of life, school, work, person's name, etc.] do you most want to celebrate today?"
- **Decision-Making**: "As we go around the circle, on a scale from one to ten, how are you feeling about this decision?" or "What additional information do we need to make a decision?" or "Which aspect of this decision are you feeling most comfortable or most uncomfortable with?"
- **Feedback**: "As we go around the circle, on a scale from one to ten, how did what I do work for you?" or "How did my handling or teaching of this work for you?" or "Which aspect of my performance are you feeling most comfortable or most uncomfortable with?"

Facilitator Completes Circle

As a way of creating a space of celebration and building energy for whenever the next circle will be, the student facilitator harvests the learning from the experience.

- **Reflection**: "In one word, how are you feeling?" or "What is one thing you'll take away?"
- **Gratitude**: "Thank you for choosing to participate," or "Thank the person on your left and right for their participation"

Post-Circle

Sometimes during a circle, something will come up that is worthy of being addressed but for which the full circle is not the ideal place to address it. In these situations, the student facilitator may need to check in with participants after the rest of the circle completes.

- **Check-In**: The student facilitator follows up privately with any participants as needed or refers participants to appropriate support resources.

Step Five: Practice Mediation Circles

Chapter 13
Creating Connection

In the Space of Connection

Where community circles help create belonging, mediation circles help create connection. One of the most powerful mediation circles I've ever witnessed was between a student and himself, and it was facilitated by a relatively inexperienced classmate. Kai, a middle schooler, was struggling with a deeply important life decision, and he wasn't sure which way to go. For him, the stakes of going either direction were incredibly high, making the decision a scary one. But his access to the tools needed to navigate this conflict was low, leaving him in a painful place of limbo. In these moments when students experience low tools and high stakes —the stress of which can contribute to self-disconnection—we shouldn't be surprised when behaviors emerge that appear incongruent with what they want for themselves (and with what we want for them).

On one hand, Kai agreed with making the decision, and on the other hand, he disagreed with making the decision. So the facilitator arranged three chairs—one for herself, one for the "agree" aspect of Kai, and one for the "disagree" aspect of him. Then she facilitated a mediation circle where he alternated between sitting in one chair and speaking from that aspect and switching to the other chair and speaking from that aspect. The effect was a mesmerizing confrontation with himself where he passionately argued one way, then the other, and then back again.

With each passing segment of the conversation, you could see the self-disconnection slowly melt away and be replaced with an emerging sense of self-connection. Distinct from the near contempt the two aspects seemed to have for each other at the beginning of the circle, an energy of empathy slowly revealed itself and with it, an outpouring of emotion. By the end of the circle, there wasn't a dry eye to be found.

Even though the student facilitating the circle was a novice, she was able to follow our specific process for mediation circles that allowed her to create a space in which the two conflictants were able to reconnect with each other and, in the space of connection, create a new path. This is what tools for maximization look like in action.

We Don't Solve Problems

The facilitator's job is to create a space where the conflictants experience connection with each other, with the belief that when they experience connection, they'll effectively navigate their own conflict. Experiencing that connection is absolutely important because if that happens within the circle, the conflictants will have practiced tools that they will be able to use in the future. In mediation circles, the facilitator's job isn't to solve the conflictants' problem. Conflictants being able to navigate their own conflicts effectively is a path to maximization.

Most of the facilitator's role is to simply have one-on-one empathic conversations with each conflictant while the other conflictant simply observes. The magic of what's happening here is that the two people who are probably not interested in talking directly to each other still wind up hearing each other and getting a sense of what's going on for the other person. Through this approach, conflictants often begin to gain a sense of empathy for each other, even without trying. What happens is the facilitator creates a space of connection with each of them individually until they start to form a sense of connection again between each other. Then, in that space of connection, they often navigate their own conflict. This method focuses on solving the disconnection that exists between them and supports the creation of a context in which they find each other again.

Through this process, two additional benefits may not be apparent to the student while participating. The first is that repeating a story or the story elements of what happened as they see it will often create freedom from the emotion attached to the conflict, enabling action rather than merely reaction. The second is that as the facilitator listens and repeats what is being said, the students can distinguish observation from interpretation, what happened from the story I tell about what happened. There is tremendous power in being able to identify what happened in the disagreement as distinct from the meaning each student has attached to it. It is logical in the heat of the moment to create your own version of what is going on and make it mean something about the other person or how you are being treated. When the interpretation can be isolated and meaning can be stripped away, it is much easier to see where connection is possible and diffuse a future conflict for both students.

The most common alternative—authority as the response to conflicts rather than connection as the response—fails to place tools in the toolboxes of our students. Mediation circle work is about putting tools in students' toolboxes. If you hold yourself up as the authority figure and you're the problem-solver, that just means next week when those students have a new problem, they're going to come back to you, the oracle of solutions, and you'll solve it for them. You're giving them fish, not teaching them to fish. This is why we train students in mediation circles.

About Mediation Circles

When conflict arises, the maximization-aligned consequence involves creating connection among the students involved. The student-led restorative practice used to accomplish connection is the mediation circle. Student-led mediation circles describe 1) conversation facilitated by students when conflict is experienced, 2) where the choice is made to use connection as the strategy for conflicts, 3) where the intention is to create and implement a mediation agreement, and 4) where the conflictants have choice and equal voice. For every one hundred student-led circles a school conducts, ideally only around fifteen of those are mediation circles. When 80 percent of the circles taking place throughout the week are focused on building a healthy learning community, there becomes a reduced need for mediation circles.

Student-led mediation circles are distinct from conflict resolution or conflict management in that resolution implies that conflict is unnatural or in need of ending, and management implies that some measure of external control must be applied to conflictants. Neither scenario would be appropriate within the context of a mediation circle. In addition, they are distinct in that students are leading the conversation rather than adults since a large part of the intention is to ensure students develop the tools they need to experience maximization.

Mediation circles are most appropriate when there are individual needs that appear to be in conflict but those needs do not rise to the level of community-wide needs, where harm has not yet been created, and where each conflictant chooses to participate. The following is one example of how a mediation circle might go. It is important that student facilitators are fully trained to lead all the following steps; they should not have to rely on adults.

Chapter 14
Implementing Mediation Circles

Pre-Circle
Before a circle can start, the facilitator needs to ensure that the circumstances are healthy for a circle to be held. The following elements should be present each time a circle is needed:

- **Conflict**: Conflict is present when two or more individuals have a disagreement or confrontation. If harm has already been created, a restorative circle might be more appropriate.
- **Co-Facilitator**: Student facilitators should never enter a circle solo. For a mediation circle, there is at least one student co-facilitator in the circle who can provide support to the student facilitator and help hold the energy to a five or below.
- **Function**: Student facilitators should collaborate with their student co-facilitators and review the referral form (if one exists) to determine what, if any, special function the circle will perform in addition to the overall benefit of creating connection. In addition to typical mediation circles, common additional functions include, but are not limited to, participants experiencing connection around:
    - **Family Group Conferencing**: Participants, including students, family members, and school officials, use the circle to work through concerns.
    - **Peacemaking**: Participants address a potential concern for which a conflict is imminent.

- o **Student/Staff Conflicts**: Participants, including students and staff, use the circle to address conflicts.
- **Disqualification**: The student facilitator needs to evaluate whether there is a conflict of interest that would disqualify them from facilitating this particular circle. Typically, that would be either because of a close relationship with one of the participants or because of the student facilitator's involvement with the situation. If a conflict of interest is identified, a new student facilitator needs to take over the circle.
- **Verification**: Is the nature of the conflict appropriate for a mediation circle? Typically, schools will have a list of circumstances for which a student-led mediation circle has not yet been deemed appropriate (usually the most severe ones).
- **Agreement**: Both of the conflictants must choose to participate in the circle. If either does not agree to participate, the process is over. In addition, all participants must be willing to grant authority over the circle to the student facilitator. If that is not the case, either a replacement student facilitator must be found or the process is over.
- **Interview**: The student facilitator meets with the conflictants to determine readiness to participate. Of particular importance, if the conflictants are at a six or above toward each other then they are, by definition, not ready to participate.
- **Logistics**: The student co-facilitator ensures that the space is appropriate for a circle and is set up for a circle and that the time, date, and location have been confirmed with all participants. Ideally the restorative leadership team will identify a space in the school where circles can routinely take place that is away from anywhere that would disturb core instruction taking place.

Circle

Facilitator Self-Connection

Student facilitators need to regulate themselves before they can create a space for community with others. While there are many techniques for accomplishing self-regulation, the tool we train on the most is self-connection practice. This is typically done silently but can be done out loud as well.

- **Awareness**: Observe Breath: The facilitator observes their breathing and gets present with themselves.
- **Acknowledgment**: Identify Feelings: The facilitator identifies the physical or emotional experience they're having in the moment.
  - Examples include "I feel..." or "The sensation in my body is..."
    - "I feel upset. My body feels tense and tight."
    - "I feel scattered and overwhelmed."
    - "I feel anxious, insecure, and not heard."
- **Acknowledgment**: Identify Needs: The facilitator identifies what met or unmet need the feeling is pointing to.
  - Examples include "I need..." or "My need for _____ is/isn't met."
    - "I need to calm myself."
    - "My need for clarity is not met around what I'm supposed to do."
    - "I need to take a break and have a chance to refocus."
- **Aligned Action**: Declare Commitment: The facilitator identifies a specific action that they can take in the moment that would be a step in the direction of meeting the unmet need or honoring the met need. Ideal commitments are SMART and can be measured or observed during the next seven days.
  - Examples include "I commit to..." or "The commitment I'm making to myself is..."
    - "I can calm myself down when I am feeling upset. I commit to using self-connection for myself the next three times I'm feeling upset."
    - "I commit to asking for directions from my teacher during the next five school days."
    - "I can control my impulses when I am tempted to act on them. I commit to stopping and taking a breath before responding the next five times John or one of his friends talks to me."

Facilitator Creates Circle

Ideally, the agreements necessary for the circle to be successful were agreed to during the pre-circle interview. But since those are done individually, it is important to reaffirm everyone's commitment to honoring the agreements now that everyone is together.

- **Prior Agreements**: "Before you got here, you agreed that you would grant me the authority to facilitate this circle, and you agreed to be open to doing the work, sometimes uncomfortable, that the circle requires."
- **Additional Agreements**: "Are there any additional agreements that you need in order to participate?" and then "Which of these do we all agree on?"
- **Check for Agreement** (and be certain to get an individual verbal confirmation from each participant): "Do you still agree to honor these agreements?"

Facilitator Interpersonal Connection

Once the circle is created, the work of creating connection with each participant begins. The intention of this phase of the circle is to create a space of connection between the student facilitator and the individual participants that will later be leveraged to create a space for connection between the conflictants.

The primary tool we teach for accomplishing this connection is the interpersonal connection practice. Where self-connection practice is focused inward and connecting with oneself, interpersonal connection practice is focused outward on connecting with someone else.

The first three steps of interpersonal connection practice continue, regardless of how long it takes, until in the student facilitator's interpretation, the participants are at a three or below toward each other. Unfortunately, the fourth step in interpersonal connection practice can't happen until participants reach that place toward each other; rushing forward before then would risk causing the entire process to collapse.

The first three steps to interpersonal connection practice are:

1. **Awareness**: Observe Participant: The facilitator observes what the participant says and reflects it back to them using their own words as an observation, not an interpretation.
    - Examples include: "What would you like to say?" or "What happened?" or "Where are you right now?"

2. **Acknowledgment**: Identify Feelings: The facilitator guesses at the physical or emotional experience the participant may be having in the moment.
   - Examples include: "Are you feeling...?" or "Did you mention feeling...?" or clarifying faux feelings.

> Faux feelings may be hard to discern; as their name suggests, they are not real emotions. We express faux feelings when we are describing how we may be interpreting the impact of another's behavior on us. "I feel disrespected by that person" is a faux feeling—it is not describing the underlying emotion (sad, embarrassed, angry) and is, instead, asserting that the other person did a bad thing.

3. **Acknowledgment**: Identify Needs: The facilitator guesses at what met or unmet need the participant's feeling may be pointing to.
   - Examples include: "Are you needing...?" or "Was your need for _____ met or unmet?"

The fourth step, Aligned Action: Declare Agreement typically requires more work before it can be done.

Restore Connection Conversation

Once participants are experiencing connection with each other—generally speaking, when they seem to be a three or lower toward each other, and not until then—the student facilitator can begin to initiate a restore conversation. These conversations are only useful when held between two people who are already experiencing connection, and they are intended to help the participants move from connection to empathy and from empathy to agreement.

- **Acknowledgment**: Connective Requests: The facilitator invites participants to begin observing—not interpreting—the comments of the other participants and to get present to the feelings that brings up in them.
   - Examples include: "What did you hear them say?" and then "How do you feel about what they said?"
- **Acknowledgment**: Restorative Requests: The facilitator invites participants to begin making requests of each other that could meet the unmet needs of each participant.

- - Examples include: "What is a request you could make of them that would meet your needs? Maybe something that begins with, 'Would you be willing to…?'"
  - A student co-facilitator should be responsible for writing so that the student facilitator can focus on facilitation.

At this point, the fourth step in interpersonal connection practice can be pursued:

4. **Aligned Action**: Declare Agreement: Once the participants arrive at agreements that everyone is willing to agree to, the student facilitator must confirm that the mediation agreement is SMART—specific, measurable, attainable, results-focused, and time-bound.
   - **Note**: If, for whatever reason, the conflictants return to being above a three toward each other, the student facilitator should likewise return to Facilitator Interpersonal Connection.

Facilitator Recesses Circle

After a mediation agreement has been created, the student facilitator temporarily suspends the circle. This is a recess, not an adjournment, because a mediation circle isn't complete until after the post-circle. So as a way of creating a space of celebration and building energy for the next week of honoring the mediation agreement, the student facilitator harvests the learning from the experience.

- **Reflection**: "In one word, how are you feeling?" or "What is one thing you'll take away?"
- **Gratitude**: "Thank you for choosing to participate," or "Thank the person on your left and right for their participation."

Post-Circle

The process is not complete until up to a week later, depending on the SMART agreements, when the student facilitator reconvenes the circle to confirm that agreements have been honored. Once the student facilitator has confirmed whether the agreements have been honored, there are three possible ways that the circle can complete: everyone honored their word, in which case a celebration is in order. Not everyone honored their word, but everyone is willing to try again, in which case a recommitment is in order. Or not everyone honored their word, and not everyone is willing to try again, in which case the circle is adjourned incomplete.

- **Celebration**: In this case, the student facilitator declares that the mediation agreement has been honored and that the circle is officially complete.
- **Recommitment**: In this case, the student facilitator essentially reruns the circle from the beginning—though it can usually speed to the restore connection conversation step. The rest of the circle process proceeds normally.
- **Incomplete**: In this case, the student facilitator declares that a mediation agreement cannot be reached and that the circle is officially incomplete. If a mediation circle is declared incomplete and the facilitator considers it worthwhile, the facilitator may opt to refer the matter to an appropriate adult for their support. Either way, the facilitator has finished their duties.

Sample: Mediation Agreement for Mediation Circles

Confidentiality Agreement

A copy of this agreement will be given to the conflictants, and a copy will be retained by the restorative leadership team. Who else needs to know?

_____
_____
_____

We agree that only the above need to know about this agreement.

Mediation Circle Agreement

We have met, discussed our conflict, and chosen the following SMART goals as ways to restore connection as much as possible:

_____
_____
_____
_____
_____
_____

We agree that the circle will reconvene on _____ to determine whether the above agreements have been honored.

Conflictant _____ Date _____
Conflictant _____ Date _____
Conflictant _____ Date _____
Conflictant _____ Date _____

Facilitator _____ Date _____
Facilitator _____ Date _____
Facilitator _____ Date _____

Step Six: Practice Restorative Circles

Chapter 15
Creating Reparation

Seed of Relationships

"Keep your kid out of my yard!" Mrs. Fells yelled at me from across her front porch. She was the block's unofficial official matriarch, and if Mrs. Fells had a problem with you, all of the older folks on the block would look at you sideways. Getting yelled at for my lack of parenting skills wasn't putting me on the best footing.

Greg looked worried as he explained to me that he had been playing with his ball in the yard when it accidentally rolled into her flower bed. Mrs. Fells took tremendous pride in her flowers; his worried expression was well warranted.

Partly due to the embarrassment that the entire situation was causing me, I found myself getting angry at Greg for screwing up so severely. On any other day, I would have gone into full-blown retribution mode and tried to think of the most memorable way that I could punish him for this error of judgment. But I had only recently gone through training on something called "restorative." It occurred to me that this could be an opportunity to test out my training. So instead of yelling or threatening with grounding, I got curious.

"What harm did your actions create for Mrs. Fells?" I asked. It felt like a strange question, and Greg was also a bit thrown off by it. But with a little bit of coaching, he eventually understood what I was asking: what had he, the author of harm, created, and what had she, the receiver of harm, experienced? He was able to describe how her flowers being knocked over might make her sad or even mad since she'd spent so much time tending to them.

> **Author**, in the context of a restorative circle, describes a person whose behavior created harm for a receiver.
>
> **Receiver**, in the context of a restorative circle, describes a person who experienced harm created by an author.

"Absolutely!" I said enthusiastically, encouraged that my training seemed to be working. "And what was the harm to our community? The harm to the people on our block?"

Again, the question seemed to throw him off, and he struggled at first. But after some light brainstorming, Greg arrived at the idea that the other older neighbors might be worried about their own yards or about disrespectful kids on their property. His logic was incredibly sound: they might worry that if this could happen to someone as feared as Mrs. Fells, it could happen to anyone. This was an insight that hadn't even occurred to me. He was picking this up faster than I was.

It didn't surprise me when he answered the next question—arguably the hardest so far—with little prompting. "What's the harm to you from your actions?" I asked. Greg responded that this could harm his reputation and that none of the older people on the block would want to keep paying him to mow their lawns. He really loved making money, and I could tell that this last realization hit home for him.

It was time for me to ask the heavy question of the process: "What could you do? What's something that you could commit to doing today or tomorrow that would begin to repair the harm to Mrs. Fells, the harm to our neighborhood, and the harm to yourself?" I asked. Greg got quiet, and I could tell he was really trying to think this through.

After a little back and forth, Greg finally came up with a novel idea all on his own: he would apologize to Mrs. Fells and offer to mow her lawn once for free as a sign of respect, and then he would go to each of the older people on the block, admit that what he did was wrong, and offer to mow each of their lawns once for free as a sign of respect.

I was absolutely stunned by his creativity! When this entire event started, my normal reaction was to yell and threaten and try to create enough retribution that he'd know never to do anything like this ever again. And that was the parental approach I had taken countless other times. Sure, usually it was pretty mild, but it was all retributive behavior nevertheless, and sometimes—if I'm being honest with myself—it was completely out of line. I had been out of control with my desire for retribution, and until that moment, I had never fully realized it.

We agreed that he would implement his plan to repair the harm that very afternoon. And so Greg went to Mrs. Fells's door and knocked. Like the coward I was when it came to all things Mrs. Fells, I stood far away on our front porch, watching from relative safety. When she opened the door, he apologized, insisted that he wouldn't let it happen again, and offered to mow her lawn as a sign of respect. She grunted, made a disbelieving face, and then closed the door. It went better than I expected.

Not discouraged, Greg began the process of going door to door to share with the other older folks on the block what he had done and that he had apologized to Mrs. Fells, and then he offered to mow their lawn once for free as a show of respect. Door after door, he had this conversation. And each time, our neighbors smiled broadly and thanked him; they appreciated that he looked them in the eye, shook their hand, and took responsibility for his actions. Some of the conversations even expanded into discussions that began to plant the seed of relationships that he'd never had with these neighbors before.

Remarkably, none of the neighbors ever took Greg up on his offer to mow their lawn once for free. But several of them did ask him to start mowing their lawns...for pay. I watched as his relationships with folks on the block improved and grew into something new in the days and weeks that followed. People would wave and call us by name when we walked past. In time, even Mrs. Fells warmed up to him, and I would see them chatting from time to time.

Low Tools, High Stakes

When a student fails a math test, we don't respond by vilifying their lack of ability and kicking them out of school. Instead, teachers respond in a reasonable and predictable manner. First they acknowledge that the student did indeed fail the math quiz and that they are responsible for learning it; it's not productive to pretend that proficiency exists where it does not or that the material will simply be skipped. Then they communicate possibility: "With your hard work and my support, you'll be able to master math." They reteach the needed material and then give the student an opportunity to retake the quiz and demonstrate what they've learned. There's nothing surprising or revolutionary about this approach to a student failing a math quiz.

Restorative circles beg the question: why don't we treat a lack of behavior tools the same way we treat a lack of math tools? Instead, when low tools are demonstrated, schools often take the most high-stakes approach they can find—up to and including uprooting students from their school community. We wouldn't default to treating low skill in math in a high-stakes way, so why is this the default with behavior?

When a student fails a "behavior quiz," instead of vilifying their lack of ability and kicking them out of school, why don't we first acknowledge that the student did indeed fail the "behavior quiz" in that moment, and then make it clear that the behavior isn't acceptable and that they will be required to be responsible for their actions? After that, we can communicate possibility: "With your hard work and my support, you'll develop the tools you need for these types of situations." Then we reteach the needed material—potentially by having them go through student-led restorative training and serving on the student-led restorative practices facilitation team. Then, as the student retakes the "behavior quiz," create opportunities for them to demonstrate what they've learned. There doesn't need to be anything surprising or revolutionary about this approach to a student failing a behavior quiz.

High Tools, Low Stakes

Part of why harmful situations end up turning into high-stakes situations is because of the nature of harm. When our agreements in our community are violated, the result is most often the experience of harm. The result is us being nudged out of our calm state of homeostasis in a manner that makes it harder to return to it. As humans, we are so deeply wired for community and community is so deeply dependent on agreements—shared commitments for behavior within a community—that when those agreements are not honored, we often feel at a complete loss for what to do. We're out of physical, emotional, and social homeostasis, often without clarity about how to find our way back. It can be easy to reach for high-stakes, retributive approaches in such moments.

Our default response to initial behavior quiz failures—and in particular, when agreements have been violated—is to create an environment where students have high access to tools in a low-stakes environment where they can gain proficiency with them. Our belief is that this is an optimal learning environment for acquiring proficiency with most new tools, regardless of tool type or student age. Much of the effectiveness of restorative circles comes from their ability to take a traditionally ultra-high-stakes situation and lower the stakes of the conversation while increasing the tools available to students in the moment. Then, as a requirement of the process, new agreements are made, and SMART goals are created to track those agreements. Such a rigorous approach to the restoration of agreements—having SMART goals attached—is an important part of repairing the harm and creating a space where participants in the process feel more willing to participate. High tools, low stakes.

About Restorative Circles

When harm has been created, the maximization-aligned consequence involves repairing the harm while supporting students as they develop the tools necessary to decrease the likelihood of the harm recurring. The student-led restorative practice used to accomplish reparation is the restorative circle. Student-led restorative circles describe 1) a conversation facilitated by students when harm has been created, 2) where the choice is made to use reparation as the consequence of harm, 3) where the intention is to create and implement a restorative agreement, and 4) where the author and the receiver of harm have choice and equal voice. For every one hundred student-led circles a school conducts, ideally only about five of those are restorative circles. When 80 percent of the circles taking place throughout the week are focused on building a healthy learning community, there becomes a reduced need for restorative circles.

Student-led restorative circles are distinct from the dominant view of school discipline, which is based on retributive discipline and criminal justice, in that traditional school discipline focuses on blame and punishment or at times views the author as an inherently bad person. Neither of these scenarios would be appropriate within the context of restorative circles. In addition, student-led restorative circles are distinct in that students, rather than adults, are leading the conversation since a large part of the intention is to ensure students develop the tools they need to experience maximization. The frequent practice that comes from leading the circles helps students mature from familiarity with the tools of maximization to fluency with them.

Restorative circles are most appropriate when an individual has experienced harm at the same time that the community has experienced harm and when both the receiver and author choose to participate. The following is one example of how a student-led restorative circle might go. It is important that student facilitators are fully trained to lead all the following steps; they should not have to rely on adults.

Chapter 16
Implementing Restorative Circles

Pre-Circle
Before a circle can start, the facilitator needs to ensure that the circumstances are healthy for a circle to be held. The following elements should be present each time a circle is needed, and in most schools, forms are created that student facilitators can use.

- **Harm**: Harm is created in a school community when an agreement is broken such that there is now a receiver of harm and an author of harm. If harm has not been created yet, a mediation circle might be more appropriate.
- **Co-Facilitators**: Student facilitators should never enter a circle solo. For a restorative circle, there are at least two student co-facilitators in the circle who can provide support to the student facilitator and help hold the energy to a five or below.
- **Function**: Student facilitators should collaborate with their student co-facilitators and review the referral form (if one exists) to determine what, if any, special function the circle will perform in addition to the overall benefit of creating repair. In addition to typical restorative circles, common additional functions include, but are not limited to, participants experiencing reparation around:
    - **Accountability**: Participants address harm that came from violating agreements that didn't violate school rules and develop a plan to repair the harm.

- o **Reintegration/Reentry**: Participants address the harm that led to separation and develop a plan for returning to be successful for all parties.
- o **Team Agreements**: Participants who are on a team together address harm that team members have created and develop a plan to repair the harm.
- **Disqualification**: The student facilitator needs to evaluate whether there is a conflict of interest that disqualifies them from facilitating this particular circle. Typically, this is either because of a close relationship with one of the participants or because of the student facilitator's involvement with the situation. If a conflict of interest is identified, a new student facilitator needs to take over the circle.
- **Verification**: Is the nature of the harm appropriate for a restorative circle? Typically, schools will have a list of violations for which a student-led restorative circle has not yet been deemed appropriate (usually the most severe ones).
- **Agreement**: The receiver and the author of harm must choose to participate in the circle, as should a student who observed the harm or was impacted by it. That third student will represent the community. If either the author or receiver does not agree to participate, the process is over. In addition, all participants must be willing to grant authority over the circle to the student facilitator. If that is not the case, either a replacement student facilitator must be found or the process is over.
- **Interview**: The student facilitator meets with the receiver and author to determine readiness to participate. Of particular importance, if the author of harm is not prepared to acknowledge that they are the author of harm or if the author and receiver are at a six or above toward each other, then they are not ready to participate.
- **Logistics**: The student co-facilitator ensures that the space is appropriate for a circle and is set up for a circle and that the time, date, and location have been confirmed with all participants. Ideally the restorative leadership team will identify a space in the school where circles can routinely take place that is away from anywhere that would disturb core instruction taking place.

Circle

Facilitator Self-Connection

Student facilitators need to regulate themselves before they can create a space for community with others. While there are many techniques for accomplishing self-regulation, the tool we train on the most is self-connection practice. This is typically done silently but can be done out loud as well.

- **Awareness**: Observe Breath: The facilitator observes their breathing and gets present with themselves.
- **Acknowledgment**: Identify Feelings: The facilitator identifies the physical or emotional experience they're having in the moment.
    - Examples include "I feel…" or "The sensation in my body is…"
        - "I feel upset. My body feels tense and tight."
        - "I feel scattered and overwhelmed."
        - "I feel anxious, insecure, and not heard."
- **Acknowledgment**: Identify Needs: The facilitator identifies what met or unmet need the feeling is pointing to.
    - Examples include "I need…" or "My need for _____ is/isn't met."
        - "I need to calm myself."
        - "My need for clarity is not met around what I'm supposed to do."
        - "I need to take a break and a chance to refocus."
- **Aligned Action**: Declare Commitment: The facilitator identifies a specific action that they can take in the moment that would be a step in the direction of meeting the unmet need or honoring the met need. Ideal commitments are SMART and can be measured or observed during the next seven days.
    - Examples include "I commit to…" or "The commitment I'm making to myself is…"
        - "I can calm myself down when I am feeling upset. I commit to using self-connection for myself the next three times I'm feeling upset."
        - "I commit to asking for directions from my teacher during the next five school days."
        - "I can control my impulses when I am tempted to act on them. I commit to stopping and taking a breath before

responding the next five times John or one of his friends talks to me."

Facilitator Creates Circle

Ideally, the agreements necessary for the circle to be successful were agreed to during the pre-circle interview. But since those are done individually, it is important to reaffirm everyone's commitment to honoring the agreements now that everyone is together.

- **Prior Agreements**: "Before you got here, you agreed that you would grant me the authority to facilitate this circle, and you agreed to be open to doing the work, sometimes uncomfortable, that the circle requires."
- **Additional Agreements**: "Are there any additional agreements that you need in order to participate?" and then "Which of these do we all agree on?"
- **Check for Agreement** (and be certain to get an individual verbal confirmation from each participant): "Do you still agree to honor these agreements?"

Facilitator Interpersonal Connection

Once the circle is created, the work of creating connection with each participant begins. The intention of this phase of the circle is to create a space of connection between the student facilitator and the individual participants that will later be leveraged to create a space for connection between the receiver of harm and the author of harm.

The primary tool we teach for accomplishing this connection is the interpersonal connection practice. Where self-connection practice is focused inward and connecting with oneself, interpersonal connection practice is focused outward on connecting with someone else.

Typically, the student facilitator will begin with the receiver of harm unless that participant chooses otherwise. After that, the student facilitator will go to the author of harm, then to the student representing the community, and then back and forth among the participants so that each of them will have an opportunity to be heard. The first three steps of interpersonal connection practice continue, regardless of how long it takes, until in the student facilitator's interpretation, the participants are three or below toward each other. Unfortunately, the fourth step in interpersonal connection practice can't take place until participants reach that place toward each other; rushing forward before then would risk causing the entire process to collapse.

The first three steps to interpersonal connection practice are:

1. **Awareness**: Observe Participant: The facilitator observes what the participant says and reflects it back to them using their own words as an observation, not an interpretation.
    - Examples include: "What would you like to say?" or "What happened?" or "Where are you right now?" and then reflecting back what the participant said, word for word.
2. **Acknowledgment**: Identify Feelings: The facilitator guesses at the physical or emotional experience the participant may be having in the moment.
    - Examples include: "Are you feeling...?" or "Did you mention feeling...?" or clarifying faux feelings.
3. **Acknowledgment**: Identify Needs: The facilitator guesses at what met or unmet need the participant's feeling may be pointing to.
    - Examples include" "Are you needing...?" or "Was your need for _____ met/unmet?"

The fourth step, Aligned Action: Declare Commitment typically requires more work before it can be done.

Repair Harm Conversation

Once participants are experiencing connection with each other—generally speaking, when they seem to be a three or below toward each other and not until then—the student facilitator can begin to initiate a reparation conversation. These conversations are only useful when held between two people who are already experiencing connection, and they are intended to help the participants move from connection to empathy and from empathy to agreement.

- **Acknowledgment**: Connective Requests: The facilitator invites participants to begin observing—not interpreting—the comments of the other participants and to get present to the feelings that brings up for themselves.
    - Examples include: "What did you hear them say?" and then "How do you feel about what they said?"

- **Acknowledgment**: Identify Harm: The facilitator invites the author of harm to get present to the harm others experience.
    - Examples include: "Author, what harm are you hearing was created for them?"
- **Acknowledgment**: Restorative Requests: The facilitator invites participants to begin making requests of each other that could repair the harm.
    - Examples include: "Receiver, what is a request you could make of them that would repair the harm? Maybe something that begins with, 'Would you be willing to...?'"
    - A student co-facilitator should be responsible for writing so that the student facilitator can focus on facilitation.

At this point, the fourth step in interpersonal connection practice can be pursued.

4. **Aligned Action**: Declare Commitment: Once the participants arrive at agreements that everyone is willing to agree to, the student facilitator must confirm that the restorative agreement is SMART—specific, measurable, attainable, results-focused, and time-bound.
    - **Note**: If, for whatever reason, the author and receiver return to being above a three toward each other, the student facilitator should return to Facilitator Interpersonal Connection.

Facilitator Recesses Circle

After making it all the way through the interpersonal connection practice and after a restorative agreement has been created, the student facilitator temporarily suspends the circle. This is a recess, not an adjournment, because a restorative circle isn't complete until after the post-circle. So as a way of creating a space of celebration and building energy for the next week of honoring the restorative agreement, the student facilitator harvests the learning from the experience.

- **Reflection**: "In one word, how are you feeling?" or "What is one thing you'll take away?"
- **Gratitude**: "Thank you for choosing to participate," or "Thank the person on your left and right for their participation."

Post-Circle

The process is not complete until up to a week later, depending on the SMART agreements, when the student facilitator reconvenes the circle to confirm that agreements have been honored. Once the student facilitator has confirmed whether the agreements have been honored, there are three possible ways that the circle can complete. First, everyone honored their word, in which case a celebration is in order. Second, not everyone honored their word, but everyone is willing to try again, in which case a recommitment is in order. Or not everyone honored their word, and not everyone is willing to try again, in which case a referral may be in order.

- **Celebration**: In this case, the student facilitator declares that the restorative agreement has been honored and that the circle is officially complete.
- **Recommitment**: In this case, the student facilitator essentially reruns the circle from the beginning—though it can usually speed to the reparation conversation. The rest of the circle process proceeds normally.
- **Referral**: In this case, the student facilitator declares that a restorative agreement cannot be reached and that the matter will be referred to the appropriate school personnel (based on the circumstances). At this point, the circle is officially complete.

Sample: Restorative Agreement for Student-led Restorative Circles

Confidentiality Agreement

A copy of this agreement will be given to the participants, and a copy will be retained by the restorative leadership team. Who else needs to know?

_____

_____

We agree that only the above need to know about this agreement.

Restorative Circle Agreement

We have met, discussed the harm, and chosen the following SMART goals as ways to repair the harm as much as possible:

_____

_____

_____

_____

_____

We agree that the circle will reconvene on _____ to determine whether the above agreements have been honored.

Receiver _____ Date _____

Receiver _____ Date _____

Receiver _____ Date _____

Author _____ Date _____

Author _____ Date _____

Community Member _____ Date _____

Community Member _____ Date _____

Facilitator _____ Date _____

Facilitator _____ Date _____

Facilitator _____ Date _____

Part III
Continuous Improvement

Chapter 17
Next Steps

Hot Flour

Once, while I was visiting with a school leader, he tried to explain to me that his school had already tried restorative practices but that they didn't work. When I hear these things, I get curious.

"What instrument did you use to measure your implementation," I asked. I end up asking questions like this in all manner of circumstances, not just related to restorative practices because the more clarity there is around implementation hiccups, the easier it tends to be to address them.

"What do you mean," he replied. The school leader had no idea what I was talking about. This is normal, so I started to ask about normal aspects of implementation – basics that are likely to transcend methodology.

"What percentage of your staff received training?" He didn't know, but guessed that maybe 4 or 5 people attended a workshop.

"Which template or framework does your school use for conducting circles?" He didn't know, but he had read a book about it.

In these moments, as coaches in this work, we are trained to be loving and non-judgmental, but also very direct. "What you're describing is like trying to bake a cake by measuring out some flour, putting it in a pan, and putting the pan in the oven. There are many more ingredients you need and if you don't have them all – each correctly measured – then that's fine, but don't expect cake. Expect hot flour."

With almost unerring predictability, I watch as some school systems will begin to implement a new strategy, do it half way, and then declare that the strategy doesn't work. This is such a common phenomenon that you will often hear school system staff refer to new strategies as the "flavor of the week." Such flavors just aren't very satisfying, though.

Getting Started

This work can be quite challenging to implement. For that reason, this chapter is devoted to helping you avoid holding a pan full of hot flour. While student-led restorative practices can be a powerful strategy for helping students acquire the tools they need for maximization and gain fluency with those tools, that doesn't mean that getting started on this journey will be easy. The six steps outlined in Chapters 4 through 16 describe how to implement this work, but they don't describe the recipe for how to go from nothing to something.

There are frequently significant roadblocks to startup, even beyond the challenges mentioned in Chapters 1 through 3. If you're trying to get this work started and all you seem to encounter is reasons that it can't be done in your school, your community, your context, or with your students, there are two strategies that can overcome those challenges: adults have their own personal experience with the work, and adults see it in order to believe it.

Probably the easiest way for people to have their own personal experience with this work is to attend a two-day orientation. School systems that are actively doing this work tend to host them regularly for their own staff and will almost certainly be open to having guests join. Alternatively, you can reach out to one of the certified coaches to come lead an orientation in your area.

Probably the easiest way for people to see it to believe it is to observe students actually leading this work. School systems that are actively doing this work may have a student training that allows observers or may have opportunities for guests to observe circles in action. There isn't really a good alternative to this; typically, seeing is believing.

Fortunately, once unwillingness is overcome, many of the key steps involved with bringing this work to life in your school are predictable. At a high level, they are:

- Create a team.
- Create a plan.
- Implement the plan.
- Capture learnings in a new plan.
- Expand from there using the new plan.

Next Steps

Creating a Startup Team

Starting an initiative like this works best when a school system-wide champion and a few school-based champions work collaboratively. Here are some common steps in creating an effective startup team:

- Identify an initiative owner from each school (the "champions") who will be responsible for guiding their schools' startup activities. We recommend starting with one to three schools—definitely no more than five—and then working out the issues before considering expansion.
    - If you don't know who the champions are yet—or better yet, you have too many potential schools to choose from—consider sending applications to your schools with the intention of identifying which have the strongest teams of champions. Start with the strongest coalitions of the willing you can find, and build from there.
- Identify a coach trained in a student-led approach to restorative practices who will guide the startup team through the process and provide examples from implementation in other states. There will be enough challenges to overcome; working with someone who can help you avoid obvious potholes will significantly increase your chances of a successful journey.
- Identify a near-term and then long-term funding source. Don't make promises to students that you don't have a plan to keep. The moment funding becomes an issue, all the promises made to students go out the window. So getting firm commitments and (preferably) the funding for both startup and five years of implementation stored in a separate account or line item upfront is vital.
- Schedule a time for the champions to attend a two-day orientation workshop if they haven't already.
- Schedule a standing every-other-week champion check-in meeting for the first six months.
- Note: During this phase, do *not* attempt to force this work on schools that do not want it, and do *not* attempt to mandate it. This work requires winning hearts and minds; you cannot successfully force restoration on a school that doesn't want it. Start with the willing, and demonstrate success. Then, going forward, only hire people who

already have a heart for restorative work. Any other approach is almost guaranteed to fail.

Creating a Pilot Plan

Host an initial meeting with the champions and the coach to discuss goals, roles, and timeline. Resources to assist with this can be found at studentledrp.org/resources. Here are some key steps in the process:

- Draft a set of SMART goals for the pilot. Remember that the primary intention of student-Led restorative practices is to support students with acquiring and gaining fluency with a specific set of tools. The secondary benefit is the impact on student outcomes for students who acquire and gain fluency with these tools. The tertiary benefit is the impact on the culture and climate of the schools. This work is primarily about maximization for students, not a way to hack a dysfunctional school that adults have created.
- Create a draft timeline and draft budget. Expect the pilot to take two to three years. A key implementation metric to build the timeline around is the student-led restorative practices implementation instrument. It can be used as a quarterly self-evaluation. Once any schools are scoring above eighty consistently, that suggests they have reached a threshold of healthy implementation for this work and are ready to recruit potential coaches to pursue certification.
- Recruit potential coaches to pursue certification. While it's great to start out working with someone external to the school system, that's not an ideal long-term solution. You'll want to immediately begin identifying interested persons who feel called to go through the certification process to become student-led restorative practices coaches.
    - Once any school system staff begin becoming certified student-led restorative practices coaches, make sure that leading this work in your school system is built into their job description. And pay them extra for it.
- Plan for development of your school system's personalized student-led restorative practices guide. We recommend taking the official student-led restorative practices guide (the official guide can be found at: http://www.StudentLedRP.org/SLRP-Guide) and again, working with a coach—creating a school system-specific version that includes policies

Next Steps

and requirements unique to your circumstances. Common considerations include:
- Drafting referral process documents for a student-led approach to restorative practices that include eligible infractions and disqualifying circumstances:
  - Behavioral Infraction Flow Chart/Decision Tree
  - Referral (electronic and paper)
  - Interview form facilitators use to determine if the referral is valid
- Drafting facilitator materials:
  - Invitation and calendar schedule for community circles
  - Sample circle agreements
  - Sample facilitator pre-circle checklists
  - Sample participant surveys
  - Sample post-circle follow up checklist
- Create a centralized data dashboard for each school to track their goals, interim goals, and quarterly self-evaluation scores.
- Create a centralized implementation calendar that includes:
  - Days of the week that students will be available to lead circles
  - Times of the day that students will be available to lead circles
  - Location in the building that students will be available to lead circles
  - Weekly practice schedule for students
  - Schedule of two-day adult workshops for the year
  - Schedule of three-day student workshops for the year
- Create a professional development plan for students and adults during the twenty-four-month pilot that's geared toward answering two questions:
  - What percentage of students in each school will be trained by the end of each year?
  - What percentage of adults in each school will be trained by the end of each year?
- Draft a list of restorative actions that could be included in a restorative agreement. Students shouldn't have to invent things completely from scratch every time; ideally, they'll have devised a menu of options to help with brainstorming—not limiting, just helping to get the ideation started.

- Draft a set of agreements, created by students, that students must agree to in order to be part of the student-led restorative practices team. These agreements should include what is required to get on the team and the conditions that would warrant pausing participation on the team or complete removal from the team. Once this is finalized, any student who wants to join the team must sign the agreement and read it aloud to their fellow students as their way of giving their word to honor the agreement. As with all restorative agreements, the agreement is either accepted by all students or it is not accepted at all (i.e., in some cases, and only for restorative purposes, the team may require additional items of an individual before agreeing to let them join the team).

Implement the Pilot Plan

It will take a minimum of two to three years to implement a meaningful pilot. Here are items to attend to during the pilot implementation:

- Complete the development of a school system-specific manual.
- Place a group of promising individuals in the aspiring student-led restorative practices coach cohort.
- Have each school-based restorative leadership team in the pilot host quarterly self-evaluations with the coach using the student-led restorative practices implementation instrument in the guide.
- Design a system for comprehensive feedback from all participants at the end of the pilot.
- Write a final report at the end of the pilot that summarizes all learnings—what worked, what didn't work, what's recommended next.

Build a Five-Year Plan

Once the system-wide and school-based restorative leadership teams are six to twelve months into a two-year pilot, it's time to plan for the future. Here are steps to consider in a five-year implementation planning process:

- Treat the last year of the pilot as year zero of the five-year plan.
- Review the team to ensure the needed people—system-wide and building-based—are at the table for a five-year implementation plan that builds on the initial learnings of the pilot.

Next Steps

- Revise school system HR practices to screen out candidates who are not open to abandoning retribution as the primary approach to behavior. If you continue hiring adults who are not committed to student maximization, this work will not work.
- Identify how many coaches will be needed to implement the five-year plan.
- Identify potential community partners who could be allies in growing this work to additional schools.
- Adjust the guide based on the pilot's final report.

Implement the Five-Year Plan

Once the pilot is complete and learning is synthesized into a revised five-year plan, it's time to pursue implementation at scale. The ideal scenario is to have the students with the most experience train the next group of younger students coming up. The more that authority for sustaining this work year over year can be placed in the hands of students, the more effective maximization efforts become. Initially, the student team may not be prepared to take on those responsibilities, but by the time you've completed the pilot, they should be.

Chapter 18
Challenges and Strategies

Implementation and Prioritization Mistakes

When a school system chooses to take a student-led approach to implementing restorative practices, those changes don't automatically happen just because the adults said so. Optimal execution requires that the restorative leadership team works to clarify the priorities and then create the conditions for implementation. Unfortunately, both of these steps—prioritization and implementation—are wrought with potential for failure.

Into this conversation come John Kotter, Pat Zigarmi, et al. They have studied and written exhaustively on change management. In doing so, they've each identified key prioritization mistakes and implementation mistakes that leaders must be vigilant against. The following is an expansion on both of their lists when viewed from the position of school systems implementing a student-led approach to restorative practices.

Zigarmi's 15 Mistakes

The Need for Change Is Not Communicated
- The first step toward change is to create a sense of urgency around why the implementation of student-led restorative practices is necessary.
- There has to be something in it for people to adopt a new practice, especially a practice that may fundamentally challenge the way they have done things.
- Leaders need to discuss the case for change so the imperative is understood. This provides a catalyst for change.

Lack of Shared Vision
- A clear picture of what you are working toward is required to share this dream.
- As the person tasked with implementation in your school, do you understand what you are working toward and how to take others along the journey?
- Beyond the school vision for the future, it is about a clear vision for change in terms of how restorative practice will assist your school in improving the imperatives that have been identified.

Lack of Alignment of Traditional/Existing Systems with Innovation
- Operating alongside or over the top of traditional values without seeking an alignment between the new way and the old way of doing things will eventually cause a problem and lead to a disconnect between what the restorative leadership team says it does and what the restorative leadership team actually does in practice.

Failure to Focus and Prioritize: Death by a Thousand Initiatives
- Innovation gone too far! A common problem for schools that have an abundance of "off the shelf" initiatives to choose from is how to embed a new initiative before embarking on the next new one.
- Schools often implement a range of initiatives and seek to implement something different each term or semester.
- In the end, staff members become reluctant to adopt any new practice because, in reality, they know that this "fad" will pass, and before long, they will be required to implement something else.
- In many cases, it's about making a clear case for change and showing how the initiatives are aligned and relate to the whole, rather than staff members seeing them as separate initiatives with no interconnecting aspects.

A Failure to Respect and Understand the Culture in Which We Are Seeking to Implement the Innovation
- It is important to understand the culture of the school before you start the change process. Is the school deeply traditional with long-standing ways of doing business that will be hard to unfreeze?
- Is it a new school just beginning to create its preferred culture? Is it a school that is already relational in its approach to problem-solving? Is it a school with a history of inadequate leadership?

Challenges and Strategies

- It is important to know what the scale of the change might need to be. This is something that is all too often ignored as implementers get frustrated with why things haven't changed in the way they had hoped.
- The other aspect that affects change tremendously is where the relationships among staff and between staff and management are not aligned.

Other Options Are Not Explored in the Experimentation and Development Phase

- Change requires experimentation and adaptation of practice to individual settings, such as working with students with special needs or younger students.
- Staff must be provided with the opportunity to experiment and to discuss what is working in terms of the application of these practices. This requires a commitment to ongoing dialogue about implementation.

Those Asked to Change Are Not Involved in the Planning

- How often have you been part of a change process where you have been told to do something different but have no say in the process? Or worse still, you find problems in the process, but your feedback is not heard or taken on board?

People Leading the Change Think That Announcing It Is Implementation

- This is a common practice with school systems, where leaders who may be enthusiastic make an announcement that this is what is going to happen, often without exposing the whole staff to the why behind their proclamation, or conduct a one-day session and expect staff to implement without dialogue.
- Of course, in most instances, this practice is less than successful, with perhaps only a handful of staff picking the new ideas up and putting them into practice.
- Whole-school change will not be possible without ongoing dialogue and a strategic approach to managing the change process. It takes time and effort to successfully embed new practice and bring about cultural change.

People's Concerns with Change Are Not Surfaced and Addressed

- If you want to fail, ignore the resisters. The restorative leadership team can learn from them and needs to involve them in differing ways. It is

important to listen to people to establish what their concerns are and to sufficiently support people in their practice development.
- One such issue raised is always around time. The time that it takes to learn, develop, and modify is real.
- While this is an investment that will ultimately save time down the track, it does take time to manage this.
- It is important that staff are supported in making this change—if they are expected to put the practice in place that they are supported in doing so.

Change Leadership Fails to Include Adopters, Resisters, and Informal Leaders
- Do not fail to sufficiently expand the field of influence to include those affected by the implementation.
- This includes those in influential positions such as year-level heads, heads of house, vice/deputy principals, principals/heads, team leaders, those in the central office, and those who are firmly against the change.

Lack of Experimentation and Adaptation
- This is believing that a one-size-fits-all implementation approach works and there is no need for experimentation.
- Innovation will not be adopted unless it can be reinvented to suit the setting.
- At the same time, this can be a trap in the sense that schools believe that their environment is unique compared to other school environments and start changing the nature of the initiative so much that the integrity is lost.

People Are Not Enabled to Develop New Skills
- People are told they will be implementing something new after being exposed to a one-day or shorter awareness-raising session.
- The provision for training and networking is not built into the budget, or access to training is restricted to certain people who may not be influential in the implementation.
- When pushing for whole-school change, it is critical to target early adopters who are expected to put the new ideas into practice and influence others.

Leaders Who Are Not Credible and Give Mixed Messages
- It is vital that the restorative leadership team is congruent in what it does and says.

- Leaders who expect one thing and do something completely different will lose credibility and greatly affect the change management process.
- This goes as far as the way leaders talk to staff and deal with difficulties within the school at all levels.

Progress Is Not Measured
- The implementation of the new initiative will soon fail if people don't know what the purpose of the change initiative is or what the school is hoping to achieve.
- Not knowing what the restorative leadership team is trying to achieve or what the progress markers are will contribute to failing to celebrate the small wins and big changes along the way. It is critical that the restorative leadership team gathers and analyzes that data along the way.

People Are Not Held Accountable for the Implementation
- All too often, schools instruct staff that this is the way they are going to do things without holding anyone to account in the process. If there is a lack of leadership and a team responsible for the implementation, the implementation will fail.

Kotter's 8 Mistakes

Allowing Complacency
- Not establishing a great enough sense of urgency—not making a clear statement that doing things the way the school currently does them is no longer acceptable.
- Not understanding or creating the need for the change.
- Not having the right person in charge to lead the change initiative or understanding that change requires a particular skill set.

Failing to Build a Powerful Guiding Coalition
- Not creating a powerful enough coalition early in the change process to help drive the change.
- Relying on one or two people to lead the change initiative.
- Not having key people in critical position on board and/or not giving them time to develop a change vision and how to achieve this.
- Underestimating the challenges of the change initiative.
- Lacking strong leadership from above to help drive the change.

Failing to Develop a Vision for Change
- Lacking a clear, simple message to understand and a big enough vision for change.
- Failing to adjust the vision as the change process is implemented, potentially altering the direction of the initiative.

Failing to Communicate the Vision for Buy-In
- Failing to lead by example and to "walk the talk," demonstrating behavior that is inconsistent with the change initiative.
- Failing to incorporate the change initiative into ongoing communication and correspondence.
- Allowing processes to remain in place when found to be inconsistent with the change initiative.
- Failing to treat people affected by the change process fairly.
- Failing to indicate whether proposed solutions align with the change initiatives.

Failing to Empower Others to Act on the Vision and to Remove Barriers
- Failing to confront and remove obstacles to the new vision.
- Allowing processes that are inconsistent with the change initiative to remain in place.
- Having leaders who refuse to change and/or make demands that are inconsistent with the change initiative.
- Failing to empower others or to hear the creative ideas that change processes generate.

Failing to Plan for and Generate Short-Term Wins
- Not systematically planning for and creating short-term wins.
Failing to have evidence of tangible change within twelve to twenty-four months.

Declaring Victory Too Soon
- Failing to have an intense urgency of change.
- Failing to understand that renewal efforts take years rather than months or a one-off session.

Failing to Anchor the New Approaches into the Culture of the School—Making It Stick
- Not anchoring change in the organization's culture ("the way we do things around here").
Removing the pressure for change before change is embedded.

- Not demonstrating how the change initiative has had a positive impact.
- Failing to employ people who personify the change initiative.

There will inevitably be challenges and pushback. Here are a few common concerns that come up and ideas on how to address them.

Staff Pushback Against Restorative / Desire for Punishment

It is incredibly common that people have only ever known a criminal justice approach to school behavior. Inside of this world view, anything that doesn't conform to the crime-punishment dyad can appear dangerous. "Where are the consequences?" people ask. The worry behind these fears is that in the absence of exclusionary punishments as the first line of response to inappropriate behavior, chaos will emerge, children will not learn how to function in a healthy manner, and the well-being of all will be put at risk by children who have no internally or externally imposed controls.

These are reasonable fears, if in fact there are no consequences for engaging in harmful behavior. What people with these fears need is clear insight into how inappropriate behavior is addressed and what the escalation process looks like. It also tends to help when it's clarified that restorative practices do not eliminate the possibility of retributive practices, but instead only migrate them away from being the first line of interventions.

It's also worth noting that school systems that implement blanket elimination of retributive practices and exclusionary discipline without first selecting alternatives—of which student-led restorative practices may be one—and implementing at least a two-year pilot as described above are most likely to both fail at implementing the alternatives and do incredible harm to students in the process.

Staff Pushback Against Student-Led Approaches and Desire for Adult Authority

As part of the student-led restorative practices implementation process, the adultism that is rampant within our educational institutions must be confronted and addressed. When adults are making choices that benefit adults at the expense of students, that can't be acceptable.

As a reminder, adult behavior that students simply don't like isn't adultism; adult authority is an outgrowth of the societal agreement about children and is intended for children's benefit.

Concern About Loss of Instructional Time

This concern is both real and legitimate. Unfortunately, most attempts to implement restorative practices—whether student-led or adult-led—allow for the inappropriate practice of displacing instructional time. School systems exist to improve student outcomes: to cause improvements in what students know and are able to do. That must always remain the first priority. It's for this reason that student-led restorative practices pull the work away from instruction and have students conduct circles in a separate space. It's certainly the case that the students involved lose some measure of instructional minutes, but if the result is that other students get to keep learning and the students who step out of class to participate in the circle avoid escalating behavior or behavior that leads to suspension or expulsion, then the net result is a significant savings of instructional minutes.

Student-led restorative practices have to be an enhancement to the instructional environment for all students, not a replacement that degrades learning opportunities for all students.

Insistence That Restorative Does Not Work

A major intention of this book and the student-led restorative practices guide is to provide schools with an implementation integrity instrument for evaluating the extent to which restorative practices have or have not been employed within the school. By having a 0-100 scale self-evaluation rubric, schools can easily identify whether the lack of results is due to restorative practices being ineffective or implementation being ineffective. It is ideal for schools, assuming they have strong support from central administration, to progress from 0 to 80+ over the course of two complete school years. Communicating this norm, combined with the restorative leadership team conducting quarterly self-evaluations, can bring comfort to those worried that there will be no measurement of effectiveness.

Parent/Family Discomfort with Restorative

Include information and permission forms about the school's restorative practices in your enrollment paperwork. The earlier you communicate with families about the school's student-led restorative practices, the better. In addition, information should be provided to all families at the beginning of each school year at any schools that are doing this work *and* families should be provided an opt-out form that allows them to exclude their child from participating in this work.

In the end, you should expect that there will always be resistance to implementing a student-led approach to restorative practices. This is healthy and natural. What matters is how you choose to lead within the context of resistance. When you encounter resistance, don't allow frustration to dominate your behaviors. Instead, try to understand where it's coming from:

- People resist being challenged about their beliefs. People believe that punishment is necessary and is likely effective. They may believe there is no meaningful alternative.
- People want to be right.
- People will resist change, even in the face of seeing the benefit of the change. They'll say it's an aberration or a lucky shot. They don't know the practice and hard work that went into pulling off that lucky shot.
- People fear that their investment will not pay off. Worse, this program will fail. Why bother to work so hard to fail?
- Schools implement new programs with promises of major benefits that never materialize. Often, schools don't put in the energy and support necessary to make something different work.
- Commitment to new strategies does not come quickly or easily.

And in the space of understanding, begin to ask yourself, "who must I become such that students have access to the tools they deserve?" Expect that this will likely involve:

- Recognizing that retributive practices are the default in our society. They aren't doing the weird thing, you are.
- Building connection and trust through honest reflection; it will produce big payoffs.
- Creating opportunities for people to opt in. Choice is powerful and freeing. It creates agency, which is very beneficial for students and adults.

- Attending to who I am being in the moment of conflict and harm. I can avoid making choices that harm what I'm trying to create. Doing so is a powerful shift in school culture.
- Acknowledging your own fears. Fear produces action, but fear is also a circumstance. You are not your circumstance. Circumstances we think are real are usually projections from something we experienced. You can separate yourself from that fear.
- Reminding people of the hard work, practice, tenacity, and joy it took to pull this off. Celebrate it. Celebrate securing for your students a powerful set of our tools they deserve.

Appendix
Additional Resources

The Framework
The student-led restorative practices implementation framework invites a reimagining of the role of schools in providing opportunities for students to learn the tools they will need to be successful in school and beyond and the role of students in creating effective learning environments. The framework pursues this by translating the existing research literature on character development, brain science, and restorative practices along with the collective experience of students and educators across the country into a set of practices that student-led restorative leadership teams can use to identify their implementation strengths and weaknesses as well as to track progress along their journey toward improving student outcomes.

It is incredibly important to me that this work spreads to wherever leaders believe it would make a difference for students. For this reason, we make all of the basic resources available for free on **www.StudentLedRP.org**.

The Instrument
This document is mentioned repeatedly throughout the book and is available on the website. We tend to update it once per year which is why I made the decision not to include it in the book.

www.StudentLedRP.org/instrument/

Becoming A Coach

This work is incredibly challenging to implement from scratch. For this reason, school systems frequently hire a coach to support this work. But commensurately, becoming a coach is its own journey.

> Learn more about coach certification at http://www.StudentLedRP.org/coach/ or email coach@StudentLedRP.org

To make an inherently challenging journey a little more achievable, we offer a cohort that aspiring coaches can join, which allows them to pursue certification in partnership with other like-minded leaders.

That said, there is virtually zero handholding in the coach certification process. Fewer than 25 percent of those who have begun the process of coach certification have earned certification. The journey from adult-led retributive focused culture or climate to a student-led restorative focused culture or climate will require effort and dedication despite adversity. Certification is no different; it's a choice each coach must make for themselves.

The Competencies

Certification as a student-led restorative coach lasts for three years. But achieving certification requires a deep understanding of the student-led restorative practices framework, the ability to demonstrate that understanding in practice, and the ability to support system-based and school-based restorative leadership teams through its implementation. These competencies are revealed through demonstrations of learning in six areas:

- **Restorative Knowledge**: what do coaches need to know about adult-led retribution and student-led restoration?
- **Restorative Skill**: what do coaches need to be able to do with this restorative knowledge and how do they demonstrate that?
- **Restorative Mindset**: through what lenses do coaches with restorative knowledge and skill see the world around them?
- **Coaching Knowledge**: what do coaches need to know about supporting schools that want to transition from adult-led retribution to student-led restoration?
- **Coaching Skill**: what do coaches need to be able to do with this coaching knowledge and how do they demonstrate that?

Appendix: Additional Resources

- **Coaching Mindset**: through what lenses do coaches with coaching knowledge and skill see the world around them?

If this journey calls to you, please don't hesitate to reach out. This vital work grows best through the stewardship of dedicated coaches willing to bring it to every school we can. If that is your calling as well, contact us.

Gratitudes

The journey toward this framework began in 2005, when a group of idealistic youth advocates collaborated on a summer leadership experience for high schoolers. Those early efforts grew into Community360, a summer experience for underserved high schoolers that focused on supporting their abilities to create the schools and communities that met their needs. Over time, the key disciplines taught became community organizing, restorative practices, and peer mediation. Many of the lessons, hard learned through those summers and through the follow-up work during the school year to support students who implemented this work in their schools, are now captured here in the framework described by this book. In addition, many more people have championed this work along the way and served as inspirations and collaborators in bringing this book to reality. None of this would be possible without significant contributions from each of the following:

Linda Amici, Korri Anderson, Jaime Aquino, Gabee Araujo, Harleigh Boldridge, Richard Carranza, Jeff Cottrill, Monica Curls, Roman Davis, Talisa Dixon, Daniel Ferman, Kayla Gilmore, Emily Goldt, Joe Gothard, Moreion Haney, Michael Hicks, Crystal Hill, Dominique Hines, Amanda Hinman, Michael Hinojosa, Kelly Isola, Susie Jackson, AJ Juraska, Celeste Kafri, Jamekia Kendrix, Greg Klein, Grenita Lathan, Janette Lindner, Lisa McCarty, Susannah McCord, Xaviera McMichael, Felicia Medellin, My Hoang Nguyen, Mike Nicholson, Clare Odegard, Debb Oliver, Myrna Orozco, LaNina Palmer, Georgina Perez, Mary Perrini, Ricardo Quinones, Steven Alan Ramsey, Mari Ritchie, Magali Rojas, Shelby Ross, Sonya Salazar, Kimberly Saunders, Renee Schultz, Lisa Shiroff, Giovana Solar, Robyne Stevenson, Laura Stout, Christine Tarrant, Janice Thomas, Sedrick A. Weaver, Bri'onna Williams, Daniel Zhool, Ray Zuniga, and the entire team at the Downtown Columbus Courtyard Marriott.

The ideas in this framework are deeply inspired by the contributions and wisdom of the following:

Ken Blanchard, Peta Blood, Carolyn Boyes-Watson, Ron Claassen, Roxanne Claassen, Sean Covey, Stephen Covey, Douglas Fisher, Nancy Frey, Bill Hansberry, Christie-Lee Hansberry, Jim Huling, Robert Kegan, John P. Kotter, Lisa Lahey, Chris McChesney, Kay Pranis, Marshall B. Rosenberg, Dominique Smith, Margaret Thorsborne, Chris Voss, Howard Zehr, and Pat Zigarmi.

About the Author

Improving student outcomes is airick journey crabill's relentless focus. His passion to improve student outcomes is rooted in his past: raised in and out of foster care, he attended eleven schools before graduating. He attended urban, suburban, and rural schools; attended private, public, and parochial schools; lived with white families and families of color; lived in racist communities and inclusive communities; experienced loving homes and homelessness. Guided by the idea that student outcomes don't change until adult behaviors change and drawing on his intimate familiarity with the triumphs and terrors of America's safety nets for children, he has devoted much of his adult life to advocating for the well-being of the United States' most vulnerable youth.

He served as Director for Community360, a summer leadership experience for high school students that focused on training students in the tools of accountability, responsibility, self-regulation, metacognition, active listening, and empathy through the use of community organizing, restorative practices, and peer mediation. He has also served as the Conservator at DeSoto (Texas) Independent School District, where, during his guidance, DeSoto made double-digit literacy gains and improved from having F ratings in areas of academics, finance, and governance to the district earning B ratings. He served as Deputy Commissioner at the Texas Education Agency where his duties included leading the deployment of restorative practices statewide. He also spearheaded reforms as Board Chair of Kansas City (Missouri) Public Schools, where, during his leadership, the school system doubled the percentage of students who are literate and numerate on grade level and, eventually, led KCPS to full accreditation for the first time in decades. crabill received the Education Commission of the States's James Bryant Conant award, which recognizes extraordinary individual contributions to education nationwide; was a finalist for CGCS' Green-Garner award, recipient of the Kansas City NAACP's Lucile H.

Bluford Special Achievement Award; received the KCPS Education Foundation's Loyalty to Scholars award.

He currently serves as senior coach with Student-Led Restorative Practices, a nationwide organization that supports schools and school systems and focuses on student maximization; senior coach with Effective School Boards, a nationwide organization that supports school boards and school board-supporting organizations at becoming intensely focused on improving student outcomes; and Director of Governance at the Council of the Great City Schools in Washington, DC, where he leads school board supports for the nation's largest urban school systems. He is the author of *Our Tools They Deserve: Why Adults Choose Retribution, How Students Can Practice Restoration*, a book focused on helping schools and school systems pursue student maximization, and *Great On Their Behalf: Why School Boards Fail, How Yours Can Be Effective*, a book focused on improving student outcomes by help school system leaders better represent the vision and values of their communities.

A former tech startup entrepreneur and avid volunteer, when crabill is not providing education leadership and coaching across the nation, he enjoys reading, coding, experimenting with flavorful and very spicy recipes in his kitchen, serving as a CASA volunteer, and zooming around on his electric unicycle. Inspired by his parents who fostered more than eighty children, crabill has mentored dozens of young people, has helped raise five young people, and will not be surprised when God sends another young person to his open door.

Made in the USA
Monee, IL
03 May 2026

49438432R00105